Henry Blackburn

Travelling in Spain in the Present Day

Henry Blackburn

Travelling in Spain in the Present Day

ISBN/EAN: 9783743314115

Manufactured in Europe, USA, Canada, Australia, Japa

Cover: Foto ©Andreas Hilbeck / pixelio.de

Manufactured and distributed by brebook publishing software (www.brebook.com)

Henry Blackburn

Travelling in Spain in the Present Day

In the Present Day.

By HENRY BLACKBURN.

LONDON:
SAMPSON LOW, SON, & MARSTON.
MILTON HOUSE, LUDGATE HILL.
1866.

LONDON: PRINTED BY W. CLOWES AND SONS, STAMFORD STREET,
AND CHARING CROSS.

To the

Rt. Hon. E. Horsman, M.P.,

In token of respect for his public worth.

This Book is inscribed, by his late

Private Secretary.

PREFACE.

The following notes of a journey through Spain, undertaken in the autumn and winter of 1864, by a party, consisting generally of two ladies and two gentlemen, may be interesting to any one wishing to know what travelling in this country is like in the present day.

The incidents related are of the most commonplace kind, the object of the author being to record simply and easily, the observations of ordinary English travellers visiting the principal cities of Spain.

It was originally intended to have published an account of the journey, almost verbatim, from a lady's diary and an artist's note-book; but in speaking of such well-known places as the 'Alhambra,' or of 'Gothic Architecture in Spain,' it was found impossible, in order to attain any measure of completeness, not to refer to such authorities as Mr. Owen Jones and Mr. Street; and to quote frequently from the Handbooks of Mr. Ford and Mr. O'Shea.

When a new book on Spain was proposed to our worthy publishers, we were met with the suggestion,—'Was there not a book on this subject by Mr. Ford?' 'There was— but it was written more than twenty years ago.'

'And had we not said that Spain was "standing still"?' The rejoinder was just, although it only expressed half a truth.

Spain is standing still, whilst other nations progress; but since the opening of railways, the number of travellers, and the desire for information, about this country and its people, have increased considerably.

In these notes we do not profess to supply the want, but only to indicate and sketch out a journey through Spain. To those who wish to 'get up the subject,' we most cordially recommend 'A Guide to Spain,' by Mr. H. O'Shea, which is, we believe, the most accurate book of reference on '*cosas de España*' ever published.

The ILLUSTRATIONS have all been taken on the spot, but we are especially indebted to Mr. John Phillip, Mr. Lundgren, and Mr. Walter Severn, for their studies from life; and also to Mr. Cooper, for the care with which he has engraved all our drawings.

Arts Club, 1st May, 1866.

The APPENDIX *contains some information that may be useful to travellers, having been corrected to May, 1866.*

CONTENTS.

		PAGE
CHAP.	I.—BAYONNE—BIARRITZ—ST. SEBASTIAN	1
,,	II.—BURGOS	14
,,	III.—BURGOS CATHEDRAL—MIRAFLORES	25
,,	IV.—MADRID	36
,,	V.—BULL-FIGHTS	63
,,	VI.—PICTURE GALLERIES, &c.	84
,,	VII.—MADRID—ARANJUEZ—TOLEDO	97
,,	VIII.—MADRID TO CORDOVA	116
,,	IX.—CORDOVA	137
,,	X.—SEVILLE	147
,,	XI.—CADIZ—MALAGA	169
,,	XII.—GRANADA	191
,,	XIII.—GRANADA TO MADRID	211
,,	XIV.—MADRID—BARCELONA—PERPIGNAN	222
,,	XV.—CONCLUSION	232
	APPENDIX	241

ILLUSTRATIONS.

'Loteria Nacionale,' by John Phillip, R.A. .	*Frontispiece.*	
Sketch in Seville, by E. Lundgren	*Vignette.*	
Map of Spain	*Precede page*	1
Burgos Cathedral	*Face page*	26
A Sketch, by John Phillip, R.A. .		42
Dominguez, the '*Espada*' . .		80
Toledo		102
Vespers, by E. Lundgren . .		114
A Sketch, by Walter Severn		128
Sketch of Cordova . . .		138
'Court of Oranges,' Cordova . .		142
Seville Cathedral		149
'Patio life,' by E. Lundgren . . .		161
Vegetation at Malaga		187
The Alhambra (from the Generaliffe)		192
Alhambra Towers by moonlight . . .		199
Moorish Ornamentation .		202
Gipsies at Granada		208
'*Caballeros*,' by E. Lundgren .		217

The ORNAMENTS *and* FINIALS *to the Chapters are facsimiles of embroidery brought from Granada.*

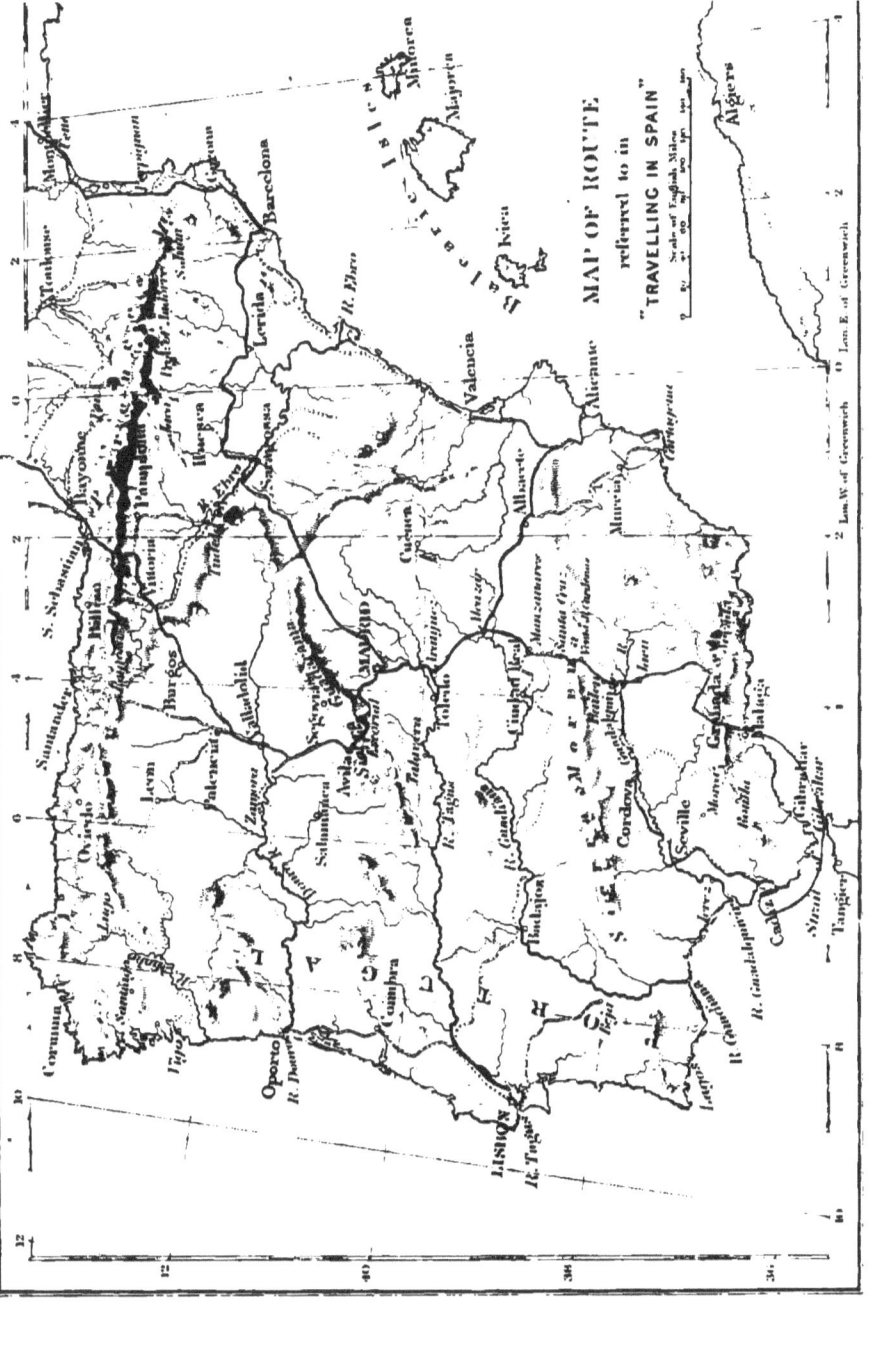

TRAVELLING IN SPAIN.

CHAPTER I.

BAYONNE BIARRITZ — ST. SEBASTIAN.

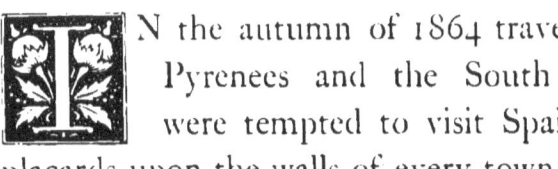N the autumn of 1864 travellers in the Pyrenees and the South of France were tempted to visit Spain, by large placards upon the walls of every town they passed through, announcing that railway communication was at last complete, and that a regular system of trains was established between Paris and Madrid.

Many of us had already had a glimpse of Spain through the wild and rugged scenery of the '*Port de Venasque*,' or the '*Cirque de Gavarnie*,' and some had visited the Bay of St. Sebastian before railways were made. But a tour through Spain, chiefly by railway, had an air of novelty about it, and a sound of promise that we longed to realize.

The project was discussed at Biarritz, where our party were staying for the sea-bathing, and it was the general opinion that, as the heat was now (the end of September) very great, the interior of Spain would be almost insufferable. We forgot, as many others had done before us, that the greater part of the country was a high plateau,[1] and that Madrid itself was 2400 feet above the level of the sea, and so we arranged to leave a portion of our 'wraps' and warm clothing in France, expecting the climate to be at least as genial as that of the North of Italy. We ought to have taken everything— more even than we had brought with us from England; a fact worth mentioning as a hint to others who may follow in our footsteps. Nothing adds so much to the comfort or discomfort of a journey through Spain as proper protection, or the want of it, from the fierce blasts of cold wind that sweep over the plains of Castile, through the streets, and up the very staircases of the houses of 'royal Madrid.'

---

[1] Burgos is nearly 3000 feet above the sea, and Segovia more than 3300.

Some of our party made visits to St. Sebastian 'as an experiment,' but on returning did not report favourably. They said that the town was 'dear and dirty,' that they 'were half-starved,' that 'there was not much to see,' and that they were 'very glad that they were not going further into Spain.' Moral.—Not to make this visit first if you have thoughts of going further south.

St. Sebastian is not a characteristic town, although in many respects more interesting and curious than any other the traveller will meet with on this side of Burgos. By 'not characteristic' we mean not Spanish, and those who have only been to St. Sebastian have seen a town that is perhaps more attractive and really picturesque than anything in Castile; but it is not Spain, and we are anxious to insist upon this, because it is here that so many of our countrymen turn back.

Seen from a distance—with its fortifications and old buildings touching the blue waters of the Bay of Biscay; the heights above studded with pretty white Basque cottages, with the pleasant contrast of red-tiled roofs and thickly wooded hills—its sunny Italian appearance is most striking. Shutting our eyes to the modern 'watering-place' aspect of part of the town, and our ears to the military band, there are quaint old buildings if we search them out, and much character and costume to be met with among the peasantry who crowd the great square, the '*Plaza de la Constitucion*,' on Sundays and holidays. The buildings generally are not remarkable, and as St. Sebastian is a favourite bathing-place both for Spaniards and French, the town is fast becoming modernized. Bull-fights are occasionally held here, but are not in vogue, and are chiefly attended by the peasantry. These exhibitions have all the rough brutality of the 'sport,' without its redeeming features of skill and courage (as seen at Madrid or Seville), the bulls being generally poor frightened animals, that would gladly escape if they could get a chance. The spectacle of the excited crowd is here, as elsewhere, by far the best part of the exhibition.

The walks about St. Sebastian, and the view from the Monte Orgullo, behind the town, are very beautiful. Accommodation for travellers is poor, and the best inn, the '*Fonda Nueva de Baraza*,' is dear, and hardly as clean as could be desired.

When we started for Spain, we decided not to stop at St. Sebastian, but to go direct to Burgos. At Bayonne and Biarritz we could obtain no reliable information about our route, nor was a copy of any Spanish railway time-table to be seen at either of these towns; we could only learn that the mail train left Biarritz about one o'clock every day, and arrived at Madrid about half-past ten on the following morning. The station-master at Bayonne could not even inform us at what time we should arrive at Burgos, nor could we ascertain this until after we had passed the frontier. We obtained some Spanish silver with difficulty at a banker's at Bayonne (it being very scarce, and no gold to be had), and on the 8th of October, 1864, left Biarritz about 1 P.M., and took the train direct for Burgos, arriving at the Spanish frontier-town of Irun in about an hour and a half, where there was a long delay whilst the luggage and passports were examined, and where all passengers changed carriages, crossing the station from the side of the '*Chemin de Fer du Midi*' to that of the '*Ferro Carril del Norte.*'

This delay and necessity for change are so characteristic of all that one meets with in Spain, that a word or two will not be out of place here on the conduct of Spanish railways generally.

Introduced by foreigners, constructed by foreign capital, and chiefly worked by Frenchmen, the Spaniards have taken a long time to reconcile themselves to this mode of travelling, and the Spanish Government at the outset took a decisive step in the way of obstruction. It decreed that, to prevent the possibility of an invasion by French locomotives and military trains in case of war, the 'gauge' or width of rails should vary from that in use in the rest of Europe! The difference is about six inches, but enough to prevent any carriages passing from one line to the other, and hence and henceforth the necessity for changing at the frontier.

The 'Ferro Carril del Norte,' being at present the only connecting line between France and Spain, between North and South, has great traffic at certain seasons of the year; but it is still in a very unfinished state, with only *one line of rails* for all traffic, every train being a goods train, with passenger-carriages in the middle. They are often obliged to travel at ten or fifteen miles an hour; and in places where it defiles between limestone cliffs and rocks in crossing the mountains between Tolosa and Vittoria, the line has been repeatedly washed away by torrents, and is continually under repair.

There are more than fifty tunnels between Irun and Madrid. The stations and buffets are tolerable, but dirty, and there is an air of poverty and irregularity about their whole system which shows plainly enough that Spaniards have not yet become accustomed or reconciled to the change of things. As there are few trains, they are always crowded, and everybody smokes with the windows closed. It is almost impossible to avoid the smoke, for, although the railway companies profess to provide separate compartments for ladies, such is the general crowding and confusion on the main lines that there is little opportunity for choice; and we must say that, whether we are travelling in Castile or Andalusia, railways do not seem to have improved the habits or manners of the inhabitants.

For some mysterious reason, no sooner does a Spaniard find himself in a railway carriage than his native courtesy and high breeding seem to desert him; he is not the man you meet on '*the Prado*,' or who is ready to divide his dinner with you on the mountain-side. He is generally, as far as our experience goes, a fat, selfish-looking bundle of cloaks and rugs, taking up more than his share of the seat, not moving to make way for you, and seldom offering any assistance or civility. He is not very clean, and smokes incessantly during the whole twenty-four hours that you may have to sit next to him, occasionally toppling over in a half-sleep, with his head upon your shoulder and his lighted cigar hanging from his mouth! He insists upon keeping the windows tightly closed, and, unless your party is a large one, you have to give way to the majority and submit to be half-suffocated.

The above was written in our note-book in 1864. Judging by the following, Mr. Sala does not seem to have found travelling more pleasant in 1866:—

'Although the Spanish railway companies are said to be doing such bad business, the trains are always inconveniently crowded, and it is exceedingly difficult to find a seat, even in a first-class carriage.

'There are reasons for this: First, the companies only run two trains a day; next, one or more first-class carriages are always reserved for government officials or taken in advance by grandees; next, the universality of smoking renders it necessary for carriages to be set apart for ladies, whether there are any ladies to travel by the train or not; next, the companies, being short of money and badly provided with rolling stock, attach as few carriages to the train as they possibly can; and, lastly, as soon as a Spaniard enters a carriage he spreads out his cloak, puts his coat on one seat and his bag on the other, pulls down the blinds, and draws the little silk curtain over the lamp, in the hope that no one else will enter. This is but natural, for we practise similarly innocent stratagems in England.

'But in Spain you are sure to be unearthed at last. You are chuckling at having entered a compartment where you can put your legs up, when you see an inquiring head and a pair of glittering eyes peering in at the window. You are found out. The door opens. A tall man appears on the steps, spreads out the wings of his coat like a bat, utters the customary *Buenas noches, caballeros*, and brings himself, his cigar, and his cloak to anchor by your side. Spaniards run to great lengths in the way of legs, and the doom of the stout is to be scrunched flat.'

There are many small discomforts and annoyances on Spanish railways which are peculiar to the country, and which the inhabitants submit to with great good-humour. They do not seem to have the art of making travelling agreeable or comfortable, and ladies must make up their minds to 'rough it,' for there is no choice. The best advice we can give them, when on a railway or diligence journey in Spain, is to take their own provisions with them in the carriage, and to remain there as quietly as possible, asking nothing about the route from strangers, or they may be easily misled.

There is not the same superintendence and system that we are accustomed to on our English lines, and travellers who depend upon being told what to do and where to go at the various stations and junctions, are continually being left behind or sent the wrong way. This is not thought much of in Spain, and amuses the officials immensely.

The '*Ferro Carril del Norte*' is in difficulties in spite of its having the monopoly of the traffic between France and Spain. The following paragraph appeared in the newspapers as lately as October, 1865 :—

'SEIZURE FOR DEBT OF A RAILWAY TRAIN.

'It appears that certain extensive iron manufacturers obtained a judgment in the Commercial Court of Paris against the North of Spain Railway Company for 4000*l*. They applied through their law officer at the Paris office for payment, but were answered that there were no funds there belonging to the North of Spain Railway. The Paris *huissier* then forwarded the judgment to a colleague at Bayonne, who, knowing that the trains belonging to the North of Spain Railway Company just pass the frontier to arrive at Hendaye (near Irun), obtained assistance and seized a train composed of six travelling carriages, besides the locomotive and tender. The whole was placed under the care of a lieutenant of the custom-house corps. The railway company at once telegraphed to their agents in Paris announcing the seizure, and the following day the amount of the judgment was paid, and the train released.'

This was sharp practice, but probably the contractor's only resource. It shows plainly enough the financial position of Spanish railway companies, and their want of credit even with their most sanguine and long-suffering friends, the French capitalists. It will account also for the poverty-stricken aspect of the stations, and almost everything connected with the line.

In Andalusia matters are much worse; the railway between Seville and Cadiz is in a state of bankruptcy, and the company have been compelled to cease running trains on several occasions, until they could borrow money to pay their servants.

But to proceed with our journey. Soon after passing the frontier we commence winding slowly up the valley of the Urumea to *Tolosa*, a small Basque town of about 8000 inhabitants. In some places the railway is carried at a great elevation, and there are here and there peeps down into far-away valleys, as in crossing the *Jura;* but both mountains and valleys are different in form and colour to any either in Switzerland or the northern Pyrenees. We passed many villages, wretched probably to live in, but looked at, at a distance, and as part of the landscape, they were charming, the old red tiles and blues and warm browns being a great relief to the eye after the monotonous grey of French buildings.

Gradually ascending the plateau or central table-land of Spain, the air soon becomes keener, the wind more violent, the cloudless sun and moon appear brighter, and as we leave the Pyrenees and the Asturian mountains behind us we leave also the life of landscape—trees, rivers, and cultivation. At *Miranda*[1] (a junction) we crossed the celebrated Bilbao and Tudela Railway, a model of which was exhibited at the London Exhibition of 1862 by our engineer, Mr. Charles Vignoles. Its extraordinary curves and gradients to ascend the Cantabrian Pyrenees to *Bilbao* are well worth seeing if time will allow, although there is not very much to attract a visitor in the town itself.

Travelling easily, in about two hours, over what a year ago took seven or eight, we arrived at BURGOS at half-past ten P.M. Here we parted from most of our fellow passengers, nearly every one of whom was going direct to Madrid.

As we only intended staying a short time at Burgos, we wished to leave our heavy luggage at the railway station, which was objected to by the officials, and, as usual, finally permitted. This performance takes place, we afterwards heard, every night; and luggage is taken very good care of; all that is required being a small fee, which certainly does not benefit the railway company. On leaving the station we experienced the most cutting and piercing cold wind from the north

---

[1] Here we were subjected to a long search for tobacco and *salt* by the custom-house officers, who seemed rather young and new to their work.

and east; so cold that we might have been travelling to St. Petersburgh rather than to the south of Europe.

The town was about half a mile from the railway station, and there was no choice of conveyances. We took the first omnibus, and for ten minutes were rattled and bumped about in the darkness, over bad roads, and no roads, and suddenly stopped at the low door of the '*Parador de las Diligencias*,' or '*Fonda Rafaela*.'

CHAPTER II.

BURGOS.

THE '*Parador de las Diligencias Generales*' is probably a good specimen of the old inns of Spain on the great high roads; constructed to accommodate a large number of people, providing them with tolerable fare at not very extortionate prices. It was, as the guide-books say, 'an old-fashioned "*parador*," decent and humble;' a rambling old building, with some of the bedrooms below the level of the road, and as we were late arrivals we were honoured with one of these.

At Burgos we experienced our first Spanish welcome; a welcome that we soon learned to take as a matter of course in our travels. Nothing can ever be done until the household come out *en masse*, and have a good stolid stare.

It was nearly twelve o'clock at night and bitterly cold, and it certainly seemed 'an age' before any one could be prevailed upon to show the weary travellers their rooms. [1] 'We were led up and down an infinite number of stairs, through dark passages, and finally under an archway into an enormous bedroom. The furniture was modern, and took up so little space that it suggested the idea of a prison cell. The windows were barred with iron, the floor was cement or stone coloured red, and the ceiling supported by massive pillars. Our next-door neighbours were mules and their drivers, whom we could hear distinctly all night, as well as the noise of rats chasing each other down the damp whitewashed walls. The very stolid Señora who lighted us down assured us that the other rooms were all occupied, and that we had the best in the Fonda. There was nothing for it, therefore, but to thank her for her attention (which she evidently expected) and to wait for the morning.'

'*Sunday, Oct. 9th.*—Our first morning in "sunny Spain." We find our cellar very dull and cold, and 'tis raining fast. Through the bars of our prison we can just see the leaden sky and part of a low barrack wall.

---

[1] Many of the passages with inverted commas are extracts from a diary, printed verbatim, in order to give the exact impressions of places visited.

'When we at last found our way out and into "*el comedor*" (a low, dingy, and most dirty *salle à manger* on the first floor, ornamented with an almanac several years old, and a few gaudy prints of saints upon the walls), we got some good chocolate and bread, and later in the day there was a table-d'hôte, to which about thirty people sat down. They were chiefly Spaniards, of all ages and degrees; and they smoked between the courses, filling the room gradually until we lost sight of our opposite neighbours. It was interesting to watch the efforts of small boys of ten or twelve to make one cigarette last out between three or four of them, smoking it in turns, and placing the damp morsel on the edge of their plates whilst they had an interlude of dinner. Other habits less tolerable and less appetising kept us on the *qui vive* throughout the meal. The fare was good for Spain (as we afterwards discovered): there were a number of dishes dressed with oil, very coarse meats, poor fruit, and wine that needed an acquired taste to appreciate. Most of our party voted the dinner "*horrible*," but that might be attributed to their insular fastidiousness or want of taste!'

It is right to mention here, for the benefit of future visitors, that this 'Fonda' is not the best in Burgos; there is another, called the '*Hôtel du Nord*,' kept by a foreigner, which might have been more to our English tastes, but travelling by the light of ancient guide-books one is often taken to the old-fashioned inns, which may, or may not, be any longer tolerable.

There are two sides to every question, and there is no doubt that in the worst inns we see more life and more that is really characteristic. It is well, perhaps, even when young English ladies are of the party, to do in Spain (with certain reservations) as Spaniards do, to stay at their *fondas* in preference to French hotels, to put up with smoke and garlic, to taste the Spanish '*olla*,' to drink wine from the skins, and (occasionally) to dine at their *tables-d'hôte*.

Spanish manners are not very refined, even at Madrid; but they form part of the sight that we come out to see.

Burgos is well described as 'dull, damp, cold, and wind-blown, and from its elevation and scarcity of trees, very much exposed to the northerly winds.' The cold lasts for seven or eight months in the year, and even in summer there is none of that softness in the air that we should expect in 42° 21' north latitude. After travelling in the south of France, and being burnt with the heat of the sun in the Pyrenees, this sudden change was as striking as it was unexpected, and we could not help thinking of our friends who had turned back at Biarritz on account of the heat.

The whole aspect of the town was so very dull and cheerless on this cold Sunday morning, and the costume of nearly every one we met in the streets so modern and familiar (Paris hats and bonnets are coming into fashion even here), that, after all we had read and expected of Burgos, we almost wished we had never come.

Could this really be the city of which we read in the ballad of 'The Cid's Wedding'?—

'Within his hall of Burgos, the King prepares the feast;
He makes his preparation for many a noble guest.
It is a joyful city, it is a gallant day,
'Tis the Campeador's wedding, and who will bide away?

Layn Calvo, the Lord Bishop, he first comes forth the gate;
Behind him comes Ruy Diaz in all his bridal state;
The crowd makes way before them as up the street they go:
For the multitude of people their steps must needs be slow.

The King had taken order that they should rear an arch
From house to house all over, in the way that they must march;
They have hung it all with lances, and shields, and glittering helms,
Brought by the Campeador from out the Moorish realms.

They have scattered olive-branches and rushes on the street,
And the ladies fling down garlands at the Campeador's feet.
With tapestry and broidery their balconies between,
To do his bridal honour, their walls the burghers screen.

They lead the bulls before them all covered o'er with trappings;
The little boys pursue them with hootings and with clappings;
The fool, with cap and bladder, upon his ass goes prancing
'Midst troops of captive maidens, with bells and cymbals dancing.

With antics and with fooleries, with shouting and with laughter,
They fill the streets of Burgos—and the Devil, he comes after;
For the King has hired the horned fiend for twenty maravedis,
And there he goes, with hoofs for toes, to terrify the ladies.'

Was it then *all* romance? Could the life and beauty of a place have so completely vanished, if it ever was anything more than a myth? 'Cold, damp, and windblown' is almost all that modern writers have to say for a city which in centuries past was one of the glories of Spain! Had the climate changed? Did the worthy citizens of Burgos go about in the month of October (as we see them now) muffled up to their eyes to keep out the keen and terrible wind? And is all this mud, damp, and dreariness a modern innovation, the result of railways and improvements which the Burgalese hates with all his heart?

But if all local colour and apparent life and gaiety have vanished, and the monotonous lines of modern buildings disappoint one at first sight, there is much that is curious and picturesque in the old narrow streets and quaint houses of the 'Gotho-Castilian period.'

The town is built on the side of a hill, in the form of a semicircle, sloping gently down to the river Arlanzon, which is crossed by three fine bridges. Remains exist of the citadel and of the old ramparts, and there are one or two Moorish archways in a good state of preservation.

The '*Calle Espolon*' is one of the principal streets facing the river, not far from our *Fonda*, but most of the buildings are modern; and it is not until we go up to the central square or market-place, with its massive arcades and old curiosity shops, that we meet with anything particularly characteristic or Castilian. Here we read that in former times public festivals and bull-fights were held, and 'lords and ladies crowded the balconies in gay attire,' and that 'the arcades were thronged with the people.' It is now a rather tumble-down looking market-place, surrounded by curiosity-shops and others, filled for the most part with trinkets and odd wares, sham Toledo blades (made in Birmingham), counterfeit coins and relics, odds and ends from all countries, but, curiously, *nothing of Spain*. We count twenty shops where they seem to sell nothing, but which are open, and their proprietors stand smoking in the doorways. Peep inside, and you will most likely see four or five figures seated round a *brazero*[1] roasting chestnuts. But it is all so dark that you cannot make out what wares they have.

One of these little shops, by the sign over the door, is a bookseller's, and we venture in. We have evidently disturbed a family party, and feel conscious of having intruded.

'What did the Señores want?'

'A Guide to Burgos—a book of any kind about Spain—or a map. Perhaps "Don Quixotte," or a rare edition of the " Cid"?—Might we look at his collection?'

A light was held by a woman whilst we hastily ran over the titles of the books that were ranged on the shelves. There were a few educational works for the use of the colleges at Burgos; one or two descriptions of the cathedral; 'The History of Cristo de Burgos;' an account of some recent religious ceremonial at the cathedral, with poor

---

[1] A large open pan of smouldering charcoal.

illustrations on wood; a Spanish drama in six acts, with marginal directions to the players as to attitude and expression, on each page; 'Cæsar's Commentaries;' and a few works of fiction, which appeared at a hasty glance to be new, and published at Burgos. There were piles of worthless-looking prints and song-books—the latter untranslatable into English—and one or two copies of an attempt at an illustrated magazine, full of advertisements of certain '*funcions*' to be held at various churches in the province of Burgos, and to all appearance very uninteresting, and a poor speculation for the proprietors.

Poor, indeed, seemed the prospect for the proud 'caballero,' who scarcely acknowledged our presence (and who, by the way, looked entirely out of place, and superior to his position), and for the group round the *brazero*, if they had to subsist on the profits of the sale of books in that little shop!

Here and elsewhere on the Plaza the people were very quiet and civil, and, if we gave no trouble and lifted anything down ourselves that we wanted to see, we were free to look about us as long as we pleased; for your Castilian, true aristocrat that he is, will lay his hand to nothing menial.

Although Burgos is the capital of the province, with a population of more than 25,000, and the seat of an archiepiscopal see, its inhabitants are not troubled with too much 'book-learning,' nor seem to be over-burdened with teaching of any kind. The shop we entered was not perhaps the best in Burgos, although a fair example.

There are one or two other booksellers: those recommended are Avila, in the '*Calle de la Paloma*,' and Rodriguez, in the '*Plazuela de Lain Calvo*;' but they are all in darkness, physical and mental.

There are numerous stores and old-clothes shops where nearly everything sold is in the modern European style. It is true that a few mantas and red sashes hang in the doorways, and we see one rusty Castilian sword and a pair of Moorish spurs; but the peasantry evidently prefer trumpery French trinkets and 'sham' jewellery, which is sold in abundance. We search in vain for some sign of industry or serious commerce, and cannot get rid of the impression that even the people themselves seem masquerading.

Spaniards seem to suffer in appearance more than any other European nation by adopting the modern costume. A swarthy, stout *Señor*, in a scanty paletòt, badly-made trowsers, and 'chimney-pot' hat, loses what he most prizes and depends upon,—his dignity of bearing; and there is no question that '*las Señoras,*' who look grand in their dark dresses and black lace mantillas (which are still *de rigueur* in the churches), do not appear to advantage in Parisian bonnets and bright colours.

CHAPTER III.

BURGOS CATHEDRAL — CONVENT OF MIRAFLORES — BURGOS TO MADRID.

THE Cathedral, the chief object of our pilgrimage to Burgos, is renowned 'as one of the finest in Europe.' As in many other cities, this noble pile is so built up against and crowded by dwellings that it is almost impossible to get any good view. But in whatever direction we approach, nothing can conceal the lofty spires, towering above the town, models of lightness, symmetry, and beauty. An old Spanish ballad speaks of the stars shining through their perforated stone, as the pride of Burgos. The effect reminds one of the tower of Strasburg, although the latter appears higher from standing alone.

Commenced in the thirteenth century, this cathedral has been modified and added to down to the sixteenth, in the style commonly called 'Renaissance.'

Our illustration is taken from a considerable elevation, and shows the west front; the only point where a good exterior view can be obtained. The architectural details are from photographs, and are as accurately drawn as was possible on a small scale.

An examination of the cathedral and its chapels, as indicated by Mr. Ford or Mr. Street, would have been a week's work, which we did not attempt; the ordinary visitor will be content probably, as we were, to be shown its chief beauties in one day. The sculpture in the chapels and on some of the monuments, the exquisite carving of figures and flowers in walnut-wood in the choir, and the general proportion and lines of the building, seemed to us most worthy of observation. The pictures are not very remarkable, as far as we were permitted to see them, but the interior was undergoing repair, and some of the chapels were covered up. The stained glass windows have nearly all been destroyed, and the flooring is at present greatly out of repair. Those who ascend to the summit of the spires will be repaid by an examination of the beautiful exterior carvings, and also of the statues which decorate its pinnacles.

Sunday, Oct. 9th.—'We spent nearly all day in the cathedral and its cloisters and chapels. We went into the sacristy, and were hurried through several rooms without being allowed time to examine their contents, but saw the wormeaten coffin of the Cid,' which is chained up against a wall. The arrangement of the choir near the centre of the cathedral has very much the effect and general appearance of Westminster Abbey, blocking up the building and obstructing the view of the interior.

There were several services during the day; the women, in black and wearing the mantilla, knelt in groups on mats on the floor at the base of the pillars; the men chiefly stood and crowded round the altars and chapels. Every group was picturesque; the kneeling figures dimly seen along the dark aisles, the men in their cloaks or mantas standing in indistinct masses, seemed to us to supply what the unknown architect probably had in his mind when he designed these naves, 200 feet long, with vaulted roofs (supported by twenty pillars), nearly 200 feet high.

The absence of all chairs and seats, and consequently the easy, natural attitudes of the worshippers, is one characteristic of Spain, and gives that solemnity and grandeur to the scene which the modern costumes, partitions, and heaps of chairs, in most European cathedrals, prevent us from obtaining.

Some of the peasantry looked as if they had stepped out of a picture by Murillo or Velasquez. One man especially we made a note of. 'He sat upon a marble tomb like an emperor, and looked as regal. He wore a coloured handkerchief bound turban-wise round his head, a Veronese-green vest, a red sash, and long quaint-shaped shoes, fastened to his feet and legs with dark sandals; his cloak was brown, lined with a plaid, which he wore in such a manner as if, unconsciously, to show the lining, throwing it over one shoulder in graceful folds. Every time he moved he fell into a grander attitude, looking like the figure on the tomb of Lorenzo de' Medici,—a poor, proud Castilian he, of the old type, little heeding that an irreverent nineteenth-century artist was taking notes of him.

Another man, whom Murillo would have delighted to honour—ragged, dirty, proud of course—the colour of an old canvas, knelt down by our side in one of the chapels, and "abstractedly" disappeared with the wide-awake hat belonging to one of our party.'

As we do not attempt a complete or technical

description of any place or building, we must here refer the reader to the guide-books for reliable details of the cathedral and its chapels. Perhaps the clearest and best description[1] is by H. O'Shea, who devotes many pages of his new 'Guide to Spain' to this subject.

One peculiarity he mentions which every one must be struck with on approaching the cathedral, viz. the 'suggestive character' of the exterior, which repeats and expresses, as in embossing, the forms of internal parts. The eye embraces the inward distribution at one glance, from the shape of the parts outside. Architects tell us that to achieve this in a work of such magnitude and variety is one of its greatest merits.

There are several fine churches in Burgos to be visited, and we are told not to omit to see the tomb of the Cid, whose bones are kept in a 'common walnut urn' in a room fitted up as a chapel in the Town Hall.

But perhaps our time will be better occupied in a drive of a few miles towards the hills which we have seen in the distance, and which are the only relief to the general flat aspect of the country, to see the tomb of Juan II. and Isabella of

---

[1] The most elaborate account is to be found in 'Gothic Architecture in Spain,' by G. E. Street. London: John Murray, 1865.

Portugal. It is here, in a Gothic church of the *Cartuja* of *Miraflores*, that we can appreciate the magnificence of carved alabaster. Two recumbent figures, raised about six feet from the ground, on a pedestal of the same material (the ground-plan of which is in the shape of a star), form one mass of carving in bold relief and most delicate imitative work. Figures of saints surround it, whilst lions and other animals crouching in different attitudes, in the recesses and niches beneath them, group boldly and effectively. The modelling of the animals is excellent, and is only surpassed in workmanship by the wonderful imitation of lace and embroidery on the figures.

Close to these monuments is the tomb of Don Alonzo, their son, around which the clustering branches of a vine are festooned upon a Gothic arch; and here again the workmanship is most elaborate.

There were other monuments and specimens of carving in the chapel, and several stained glass windows; but all the riches and magnificence crowded together here, could not dissipate the desolate air of everything about this almost deserted convent.

It was sad to walk in the lonely cloisters and hear from the poor monks (the two or three remaining ones who conduct strangers over the convent) what the '*Miraflores*' must once have been, and suggestive as a contrast, after the alabaster tombs of kings, to visit the '*champ de repos*' of 419 Carthusian monks 'who lie here in death, as they lived, humble and forgotten, without a name or a date, amongst the weeds, shaded by tall and sombre cypresses, which raise their arrowy, motionless spires to heaven.'

Quitting Burgos at half-past ten at night, we went direct to Madrid, leaving behind us three cities that especially ought to be visited: *Leon* for its cathedral, *Valladolid* for its sculpture and historical associations, and *Segovia* for its architecture and picturesque site. Leon is now to be reached by railway, leaving the main line at Venta de Banos. Valladolid is one of the principal stations, at which we arrive two hours after leaving Burgos. Segovia is more easily visited from Madrid.

These three towns contain more antiquities, and are richer in specimens of early Gothic architecture, than almost any others in Spain. Mr. Street devotes a large portion of his book to a description of their cathedrals and monuments, and, although the accommodation is rather primitive, the traveller will be well rewarded for exploring them all, but especially Segovia. Information about the journey to these towns will be found in the APPENDIX.

'A very lovely sunrise, the next morning, over the Guadarama mountains, presenting one of those strange bright contrasts between the deep-red glow of the waving lines of hills, and the cold, clear, blue sky, that is seldom seen in any other country. It was just that effect that Holman Hunt strove to render in his picture of "the Scapegoat" dying on the salt sand of the Dead Sea, and that later, was so much criticised in a drawing by Telbin of the mountains by the Sea of Galilee.

'Warmth of colour, and cold photographic hardness—almost harshness—of form and outline, with a background of the most tender delicate blue.'

At this part of our journey we might have been in the East, for all the signs of life or vegetation that could be seen; nothing but ridges of brown, barren mountains, rising one behind the other in dreary monotony; no towns, no villages of any importance, and hardly any inhabitants.

There are fifty-seven tunnels between Irun and Madrid, and the railway winds in and out between the mountain ranges, keeping an average level of

1500 feet above the sea. As we approach Madrid there are more signs of cultivation, and we pass first something that looks like a farm, and then a manufactory with a chimney that reminds one of Manchester—the style of architecture is unmistakable.

About 9 A.M. we pass the '*Escorial*,' the tomb of the Spanish kings, and soon after 10 A.M. arrive at Madrid.

We are late, of course. The 'curves' and 'gradients' that we have passed over during the night are not favourable to a high rate of speed, and we are fortunate if we average more than eighteen miles an hour. The time wasted at stations where there were no passengers, or any sign of a town; the listless way of doing everything connected with the traffic, and the national hatred of punctuality, all tend to the same end. Matters do not seem to improve, judging from a letter from a passenger by the 'express' train in November, 1865, who writes of this part of the journey,—'On we plodded, up hill and down hill, as if drawn by short-winded and broken-kneed engines, the very dogs coming out, running along and barking at us in front and in rear, doubling us round and round as if we were some old *patache*, with which they could keep up races at will.'

The fact is, that we are really travelling by the luggage-train, and that, owing to the poverty of the system of *one line of rails* for all traffic, the train is composed chiefly of cattle and goods trucks, which we have to 'shunt' and take up at the various small stations, and which sometimes reach to an enormous length, with two or three passenger-carriages in the middle. In winter, on steep gradients and with frequent snow on the Guadarama mountains, it is almost impossible to keep correct time, as one unpunctual train disarranges the whole system for the day or longer.

In spring and autumn the traffic is greater than the railway company can properly undertake, and much crowding, discomfort, and delay, is the consequence: and all this on a line which at other times has not sufficient funds to pay its working expenses, and has never paid for its construction. Before reaching Madrid we passed the *débris* of a train that had been smashed to pieces in a collision two days before. The fragments of carriages and of twisted rails remained in a huge pile at the road-side, no one having taken the trouble to remove or conceal them.

The Custom-house visitation at Madrid is much more troublesome than at the frontier, and often causes vexatious delays. When we arrived here for the first time, a reception at the palace was to take place on the following day, to which numerous foreigners were invited: the result was that court dresses, and others that had scarcely been used, had to go through a severe scrutiny, and their owners cross-questioned as to their having ever been worn. Woe to those ladies who had packed carefully, and whose dresses were in a good state of preservation! They had to pay about one guinea each, or leave their portmanteaus at the Custom-house!

As passengers by this train have generally been travelling day and night from the frontier, they are not in a humour to attempt to resist the extortion, and so the system flourishes to this day.

CHAPTER IV.

MADRID.

VERY traveller goes at once to the 'Puerta del Sol,' the great central '*place*,' the life and heart of Madrid.

From our window in the '*Fonda de los Principes*' we look down upon a bright and brilliant scene, unlike anything in any other capital in Europe. The houses and public buildings are, it is true, of no particular style of architecture, and the shops and their contents are more Parisian than Spanish; but in spite of the prevailing modern European style of dress, there is colour and variety of costume in the crowd. The mantilla is still occasionally worn, and Spaniards of all degrees take care to display the gay-coloured silk linings to their cloaks; there are the tassels and bright worsted trappings to the mules, and the quaint dresses of the water-carriers continually passing with their loads: detachments of troops are moving about in every direction, and the crowd is greater than on the Paris Boulevards.

All the principal streets lead into or towards this spot, where there is constant traffic night and day. The 'Puerta del Sol' is about 400 feet in length north and south, by about 150 feet wide, being rather narrower at either end.[1] The building which occupies the western side is the *Palacio del Gobernacion*,' the Home Office, and also the central depôt for troops. Opposite are shops, with one or two of the principal hotels above. The south end is formed by the newly-erected '*Hôtel de Paris*,' with the *Calle de Alcalá* and the *Carrera de Geronimo* (two fine streets leading to the Prado and the Southern Railway Station) on each side. On the north are private houses, with other streets — the *Calle Mayor*, and the *Calle del Arsenal* — leading to the Palace, the public gardens, the river Manzanares, and the Northern Railway.

Six other streets converge upon the ' Puerta del Sol' (the Gate of the Sun), and seem to

---

[1] The ' Puerta del Sol ' is so often referred to in books of travels in Spain, that we had prepared an illustration of it: but the details were all modern, commonplace, and uninteresting, and the whole when completed looked so much more like (what a lively writer lately compared it to) an exaggerated sketch of ' Seven Dials,' in St. Giles's, London, that we were obliged to discard it.

draw, irresistibly, almost all the traffic of the city towards this one spot; and as the Madrileños are more alive by night than by day, the noise and movement seem incessant to any one unaccustomed to the place.

'There is a fine fountain in the centre of the " Puerta" well supplied with water, which is now playing, as we write, at least sixty feet high, flashing in the moonlight, and giving that bright aspect to the place which strikes every visitor. The pavements are broad under our windows, and at twelve o'clock to-night there are at least five hundred people standing about or *en promenade*.'

We remarked that few people left the pavement or stood in the centre of the square, but were unaware at the time that there was a regulation (of which the disturbances in January, 1866, showed the necessity) which prohibited groups of persons standing together in the centre of the square.

We read that Madrid, which in 1857 had about 290,000 inhabitants, 'contains upwards of 8000 houses, 146 churches and other religious buildings, 88 squares and plazas, 33 fountains, and 50 public wells.' But we learn from residents that since the above was written Madrid has greatly increased in population and in houses, and is also improved in its sanitary condition. The inhabitants owe their plentiful supply of water to the exertions of foreign engineers, who in different parts of Spain are constructing over again for the Spaniards works which the Moors had already made for them, and which they had wantonly destroyed, or allowed to go to ruin.

It is difficult to obtain a good general idea of Madrid at first sight, as there is no high ground near the centre from which to look down upon the city. There is only one distant view of the Guadarama mountains looking over the river from the square in front of the palace, northwards towards Segovia. The scene is stern and desolate-looking to unaccustomed eyes, but at sunrise and sunset there are often very beautiful effects from this terrace; and if artists, who have almost given up Madrid as hopeless, will stroll out by the Toledo Gate towards evening, and, getting on the high ground near the English cemetery, look back upon the city as the sun goes down, they will sometimes see its towers and spires glowing in a golden light, seldom seen north of Africa.

Madrid is about eight miles round, but the environs are not interesting, and the roads are badly kept. We no sooner go out by any of the gates than we feel irresistibly drawn back to the city, and to its centre, the 'Puerta del Sol.'

The Spaniards we know have been backward enough in adopting modern improvements. They dislike railways particularly, because they compel them to be tolerably punctual; they do not object to steam in the abstract, because it saves trouble, and they have here in the capital permitted foreign nations to do much to make this 'city set upon a hill' healthy, habitable, and tolerably comfortable. Pure water brought from the Guadarama mountains flows everywhere, and trees and flowers flourish, in the principal streets, which are generally well kept and clean, with good pavements for foot passengers. The shops are filled with French goods, the best being kept by French people, and there is little that is Spanish to purchase, or even to attract the notice of a stranger.

On the '*Prado*' and the '*Fuente Castellana*,' the chief afternoon promenades, an Englishman will be struck with the style of the carriages, and with the number of 'thoroughbreds' that pass up and down over the half-mile of straight drive, although the 'handling' is of course after the manner of the '*Bois de Boulogne.*' It is not fashionable to walk anywhere: it is even thought better to sit in a closed cab which jolts you terribly, at the rate of four reals (less than one shilling) an hour, over the rough stones on their roadways.

Every day whilst we have been here some of the royal family drive past our hotel on the 'Puerta del Sol' in closed carriages drawn by six mules with gay trappings. Their approach, long before the carriages are in sight, is heralded by a faint squeak from something between a penny trumpet and a French horn, issuing from the gate of the '*Palazzo del Gobernacion.*' The number of squeaks is regulated according to rank, thus:— three squeaks for the Queen, two for the Infanta, one for the Queen's mother, and so on. There is a perpetual interchange of visits between Queen Isabella and the Queen-Mother, who live at opposite sides of the city, and call on each other every day. The cradle and perambulator follow on these visits in an open carriage, drawn by four mules with outriders and attendants. It is the event of the afternoon for a stranger, when resting after a heavy morning's work at the picture galleries, to see the royal carriages pass to and fro, though we must confess to having somewhat wearied of the penny trumpet.

We should not omit to make mention here of

the '*Guardias Civiles*' (Civil Guards) that we see constantly on duty about the Palace and the Government offices. Through the kindness of Mr. Phillip we are enabled to give a lifelike sketch of one of them, lounging about near the 'Puerta del Sol' in his picturesque uniform. They are a fine body of picked men (like the Irish constabulary), the representatives of public order, the prop and stay of the Government, whatever party may be in power. We shall see them constantly in Andalusia, riding about the country, with their long cloaks covering both horse and man.

Madrid is described in every handbook and book of travels, and the accounts vary very little. What was true of it when Ford wrote is nearly true to-day. One of the best descriptions appeared in the 'Times' in November, 1865, from which we will make one or two extracts for the benefit of our readers.

The following will give some idea of its climate, and its recommendations as a place of residence at the present time:—

'Those who have seen anything of Spain beyond the Pyrenees must be fain to confess that *Madrid is one of the least interesting cities, situated in one of the most unfavourable spots, and subject to one of the most trying climates upon earth.*

'The spot on which this town was laid, the desert over which Madrid is said to lord it (*Madrid che signo-*

reggia in un deserto), never looked to greater advantage than it does at this present moment. The rains which have flooded the southern provinces, which have broken down bridges and embankments of the Andalusian railways, have only fertilised and revived the parched-up " tawny " plain of Castile.

'Seen from some of the swelling waves with which the land is diversified, as from the terraces of the Queen's plain yet stately Palace, or from the Royal Observatory, the treeless, hedgeless champaign just now looks less dreary and desolate, and the range of the Guadarama mountains, with the sunset upon it, fills us with a gladness which convinces us that Madrid is not, after all, so utterly Godforsaken a spot as it is described.

' The promenades, or *paseos*, which run nearly all round the town, with the exception of the " Prado" and "Fuente Castellana," are in a most deplorable state of neglect, flanked with stunted, shaggy trees, furrowed with deep ruts, a sea of mud, impracticable for men or beasts, unfit either for walking or driving, as is, indeed, too generally, the town pavement. Those fashionable bits on which the people move round and round, like horses in a mill, and at a funereal pace, lie low and have no view ; and the same may be said of the "Retiro," and of some other Royal *delicias* occasionally open to the public, while the only commanding ground, the " Montana del Principe Pio," has been sadly cut up and laid waste, to make room for a huge pile of barracks, an eyesore to the country far and wide, and an obstruction to part of the glorious prospect opening before the windows of the Queen's Palace.

' On the whole, if the site of Madrid was naturally no great thing, it is impossible to deny that hardly less could be made of it than has been made. The sky, however, is very fine indeed when fine, and I hardly know any spot on the favoured Mediterranean where so calm and mellow, as well as bright a sunset could be enjoyed as we had here last evening. I know no spot in dear Italy encompassed by so pure, deep, translucent a canopy of heaven as gladdens our heart now, at this moment I am writing.

'There are drawbacks to this ineffable enjoyment, no doubt, and whatever may be said of the qualities of the Madrid climate, and of its good effects on Charles V.'s gout, we cannot forget that the town lies at an altitude of 2400 feet above the sea-level. The air is keen, bracing with a vengeance, and the contrast between the warm sultry day and the sharp frosty night puts a man's endurance to the direst test, even when the atmosphere is perfectly still, as it now is, even when the boisterous, murderous north blast does not sweep irresistibly over the devoted plain.

'Cold as it is in the earliest and latest hours of the day, we would scarcely feel disposed to call the present season "winter," though we find our bright chimney corner the pleasantest, and, in every sense, *dearest* spot in Madrid. The people that go about the streets, however, seem to look upon their country as another Siberia. The newspapers have gravely been warning their readers for the last fortnight that it is necessary "*taparse, y taparse bien,*"—to muffle up, and muffle up tightly; and it is hardly credible what amount of capes, comforters, and other wrappers, old and young contrive to load themselves with. People of all ages (however, hardly of both sexes, for the women walk bareheaded, or, at the utmost, slightly shaded by the veil of the mantilla, which is but a poor apology for a head-dress) go about *embozados*, wrapped up to their very noses, creeping at a snail's pace, encumbering the narrow side-walks, till a man accustomed to the rapid tide of the London or Paris thoroughfares frets himself to death, and feels tempted to make his way through the sluggish crowds by jumping over their heads, or knocking them down right and left!'

This is Madrid 'in the present day.' In the cosy little reading-room of the '*Hôtel de Paris*,' or at the 'Casino,' you may any day meet a group of foreigners echoing the same sentiments, equally puzzled and pleased with Madrid. Pleased with its brightness, gaiety, and sparkle, with the hospitality and kindness they have met with: puzzled with the strange mixture and contradiction in the character of its inhabitants; and annoyed at their want of system, their inertness and laziness, and especially at the exorbitant prices of everything in and near the capital.

The fact is, that if, as we have said, the Spaniards are slow to adopt the habits of neighbouring countries, they seem to have grasped at one of the vices of weak nations—over-centralisation. It is this that makes living so expensive, and raises the rent of an attic on the Puerta del Sol to 150*l.* a year. Every one strives to live as near as possible to the centre, and house-rent within a radius of half a mile is dearer than in London or Paris.

Madame Simon excused the enormous charges in her bill at the '*Fonda de los Principes*' by stating the rent she had to pay for two or three upper floors—a sum that we should be afraid to repeat for fear of seeming to exaggerate. Prices are still on the increase, and it will soon be almost impossible to reside near the Puerta del Sol.

A glance at the map of Spain will show the reason, and how central the capital is, both by its natural position and the formation of roads and railways. In a very short time railways will be completed giving Madrid an unexampled situation, with the port of Bordeaux on the north, Lisbon on the west, Cadiz on the south, and Barcelona on the east, all in direct communication by railway with the capital,—its centre the *Puerta del Sol.*

Everything is brought to the capital, and every one must go to the capital to supply his most ordinary wants. There is hardly any means of communication or any road in Spain that does not lead to Madrid. The adventures of a gentleman who journeyed from Oporto to Salamanca as lately as December, 1865, and an account of which appeared in the newspapers at that time, gave a good idea of what travelling on cross roads is like since the introduction of railways.

If the traveller when he enters Spain may be likened to a fly which has just stepped into a spider's web and must take the consequences, in Madrid he has arrived at the centre, and his enemy is upon him. There is no escape, he must pay and pay. Twenty-five shillings a day, and even more in the height of the season, it costs each person in the large hotels for poor rooms and very indifferent fare. We are not very partial to the system of monster hotels, where there is no host to welcome you or to care for your wants, where no one troubles himself whether you go or stay, and where you feel from the moment you enter that you are part of a huge machine. But in Spain 'everything goes by contraries,' and the '*Grand Hôtel de Paris*' at Madrid is like a drop of water in a thirsty land. It is the one only spot in all Spain where a stranger can find really good accommodation. He must pay for it, as we have said before, but in this instance there is 'quid pro quo.'

Since the opening of railways, and the great increase of visitors to Madrid, the old hotels have been found quite insufficient, and French capitalists supplied the want. They built a '*Grand Hôtel*,' and, receiving their supplies daily from Bayonne and Paris (and even we were told from Billingsgate), provide the Spaniard, who would never have done this for himself, with most of the luxuries of the French capital. All nations congregate here of course, and in the season it is difficult to get rooms at any price.

In keeping with everything Spanish, followers of 'Murray,' and, strange to say, of our universal 'cicerone' 'Bradshaw,' were, until very lately, directed, on arriving at Madrid, to go first to the '*Fonda da Inglaterra*,' which has long been closed, and next to the '*Fonda de los Principes*,' which is very inferior to the '*Hôtel de Paris*.' We speak from experience, having stayed some time at both of them.

At the '*Fonda de los Principes*' we had good rooms in the front (on the fourth floor), lofty, and tolerably well furnished after the French fashion; but the living was bad, and the most expensive wines tasted so strongly of the skins that it took some days to get acclimatized. We paid at the rate of one guinea a day for each person, without a sitting-room, and this did not include '*service*.' No one seemed to care whether we stayed or not. The hotel was crowded and dirty, and the attendance—Spanish.

To quote from our diary :—

'Our beds are made by a dirty, goodnatured little man, who sits upon them and smokes at intervals during the process. Our fellow-travellers, who have been much in Spain and have been staying here some time, say that he is one of the best and most obliging servants they have met with. He attends to all the families on our *étage*, and earns eighteen or twenty shillings a day! Every one has to fee him, or he will not work. We found him active enough until the end of the week, when our "tip" of sixty or seventy reals, equal to about two shillings a day, was indignantly returned as insufficient and degrading. The latter was the grievance; his pride was hurt, and we never got on well afterwards. He had a knack of leaving behind him the damp, smouldering ends of his cigarettes; and on one occasion, on being suddenly called out of the room, quietly deposited the morsel on the edge of one of our plates on the breakfast-table!'

The above is one—out of 'a thousand and one' eccentricities—which we should not have thought it worth while to note but that we are writing for the information of those who wish to know how far the Spain of to-day resembles in the habits of the people the Spain of Ford. In all the small details of travel and hotel life the Spaniards seem to have changed little. A lady cannot in the year 1866 sit down to a *table-d'hôte* in Madrid without the chance of having smoke puffed across the table in her face all dinner-time; her next neighbour (if a Spaniard) will think nothing of reaching in front of her for what he requires, and greedily securing the best of everything for himself.

'That is an educated gentleman opposite, but he has peculiar views about the uses of knives and forks; next to him are two ladies (of some position, we may assume: they have come to Madrid to be presented at the levée to-morrow), but their manners at table are simply atrocious.'

We will say nothing about one or two delicately-rolled '*cigaritos*' between taper fingers; but when we see these señoras take up half the dessert off the dishes, and walk out of the *salle à manger* with wooden toothpicks sticking out of their mouths, we can hardly wonder at Mr. Sala (writing from this very hotel) saying:

'I wouldn't bring my maiden aunt; I wouldn't bring my spinster cousin; I wouldn't bring any lady (unless she were another Ida Pfeiffer or Lady Hester Stanhope) to the town, or the inn, or the room in which I am now dwelling.

'Spain is full of beauties which the lover of the picturesque might glory in, but it is equally full of horrors which would appal the mere child of civilization.'

This is the traveller's experience in hotels. If he goes into society, it is only amongst the few that he meets with the same amount of cultivation and refinement that he is accustomed to at home. The average Spaniard reads little, and is, as a rule, still very ignorant. He is courteous in his own way, and courtly by nature; very kind and hospitable in entertaining strangers, but (it seemed to us) rather bored by visits even of his own countrymen, and happier amongst his own set.

Without discussing the Spanish character or attempting any analysis, speaking only of what came under our notice, we should add that we found the Spaniards 'at home' much more cordial, kind, and hospitable, than we had been led to expect by their conduct abroad; and that in their home-life and in the education of their children they seemed to be adopting many of the habits of more northern nations, and falling in with 'views' which a few years ago would have been scouted. They are slow to admit this, but in the matter of education especially there is no doubt that the next generation will show a great advance.[1]

In the common out-door life of Madrid, Paris is copied, and, if it were not for the unmistakable Spanish faces, the crowd '*en promenade*' might be Parisian. Their horses are splendid, their car-

---

[1] There are a number of English and Scotch governesses in Madrid, and English educational works are now openly allowed to be sold.

riages are English-built, and both 'four-in-hands' and 'tandems' are seen on the Prado.

But there is one special characteristic in the crowd under our hotel-windows, a crowd that never disperses day or night. It is in the number of idlers, of men standing about from morning till night wrapped in cloaks. The majority are, to tell the truth, an ill-looking set, have a low type of face, a slouching aspect, and an ill-mannered address if spoken to. They loiter in all the frequented places in Madrid, and are very much in the way. They hardly speak to one another, and scarcely seem to have energy enough to light a cigarette, scratching their fusees sometimes (as we have seen them) on the coat of a passer-by, in a contemplative, patronising fashion, that takes a stranger rather aback.

A young Madrileño is content to lounge his life away in this fashion; and if he has an income sufficient to keep him in '*cigaritos*,' to pay for his weekly seat at the '*Plaza del Toros*,' and to provide him the bare means of subsistence, he will do no work. He is ready in case of an *émeute*, or for a place under Government —neither would come amiss to him. It is all he seems fitted for, and apparently the height of his ambition. In the morning a lounge on the 'Puerta del Sol,' in the afternoon a walk or ride on the 'Prado,' in the evening to a café or theatre, varied occasionally by a bull-fight or a cock-fight—is the average employment of half the young men in Madrid. There is not much betting, or 'sporting' in our sense of the word, even at the bull-fights, and they seemed to us on most occasions to do what Englishmen alone have been accused of, 'to take their pleasure sadly.'

It was amongst such a crowd as we have described—careless, listless apparently, and yet excitable, not too well affected towards the royal house—that Queen Isabella made her last public entry into Madrid on the 14th of December, 1865; and it was to such a crowd, apparently unmoved and unconcerned, that martial law was proclaimed to the sound of the trumpet on the 3rd of January, 1866. The bells rang out when the Queen entered Madrid; but the population were silent, and barely greeted her. Drums beat loudly and trumpets sounded, O'Donnell marshalled his troops on the Puerta del Sol, and reports of the rising of the population reached Madrid every hour; but still that curious quiet crowd stood about the square, as it had done any time these forty years, and made no sign.

The women seem more cheerful and industrious, although we see comparatively few in the streets. In the early mornings they go in great numbers to the various churches, dressed in black and wearing the mantilla, but in the afternoon, bright, if not tawdry colours, are the '*mode*,' and Spanish features and complexions are put through the forcing process of wearing Parisian bonnets with a result hardly successful in the eyes of foreigners.

In every guide-book to Spain we are told that black dresses are generally worn by ladies, and that it is better for strangers to follow their example. We can only say that we have found black *seldom* worn excepting in the churches, and that an ordinary quiet travelling costume excited the least attention. The sorrows and trials of a lady who travelled through Spain alone wearing a hat have been made the subject of a volume;[1] but then the Spaniards, who have quietly put up with a great many innovations by foreigners, have not yet reconciled themselves to the idea of a lady travelling third class and alone, with a dog, from one end of Spain to another. It is the right way to see the country no doubt, and those who travel

---

[1] 'Over the Pyrenees into Spain.' by Mary Eyre. London. Bentley, 1865.

more luxuriously miss much that they ought to see; but in Spain it is not customary for any lady to travel unattended, and it is not extraordinary that she 'came to grief.'

In a few years all this must change. In the crowd under our windows, whilst we are writing, we could point out almost as many foreigners as Spaniards, and a stranger is no longer a 'rara avis,' or anything to be wondered at. It is true that in this year (1864) the Exhibition at Bayonne, the opening of the railway to France, and the presence of the Court, has attracted an unusual number of strangers to Madrid at one time, and the town is acknowledged by every one to be exceptionally full. Nevertheless we cannot but think that a great change is coming over the 'Madrileños,' if not over Spaniards generally, and that foreigners will soon be welcomed to the capital.

The above, written in November, 1864, is hardly borne out by the more recent experience of the 'Times' correspondent writing on January 1, 1866, which we print on the next page.[1]

---

[1] We have inserted several extracts from newspapers, because they are valuable in bringing the information down to a later date, and give the reader an assurance (whether such assurance be needed or not) that our picture of 'Spain in the present day' is neither exaggerated nor taken from one point of view.

'The Spaniards have their capital very nearly all to themselves. The hotels begin to be crowded; but it is with commercial travellers chiefly, with Opera dancers and singers, railway engineers and contractors. The infrequency of strangers, of mere holiday visitors and pleasure-seekers, such as flock at this time of the year to Nice, Florence, or Naples, greatly astonishes, though it by no means distresses the natives, who, if they have not travelled at all, or only a little, are apt to look upon Madrid as the most attractive spot on the face of the globe.

'To say nothing of the undeniable fact that the place is too cold in winter, and too hot in summer; that it was till the Great Northern line was opened one of the least accessible cities in Europe, and that even the present railway arrangements are among those " things of Spain" at which foreigners are proverbially disposed to grumble,—to say nothing of all that, there is no getting over the point that when you have been at all the trouble of travelling to Madrid you find that there is not much, if anything, worth coming for; that the town has barely anything to boast of except the Queen's Palace, which is not to be seen, and where there is nothing to see, and the Museo, or Picture Gallery, which, indeed, overwhelms your mind by its countless treasures of art, but which also wrings your heart by the exhibition of some of poor Raphael's masterpieces, blushing brick-red with the daub of the sacrilegious restorer, and sends you back with such sorrow and wrath at the irreparable loss of the "Perla" and "Spasmo di Sicilia," as to leave hardly any agreeable impression from the square acres of canvas that Titian, Murillo, and Velasquez have here put together for your gratification.

'Yet, although it is not much of a capital, and although for the lovers of history and antiquity it is not very Spanish, there is enough that is odd and peculiar to keep alive a stranger's interest for a few days.

'On a first cursory glance at the streets of Madrid, it would seem that there are none but carriage company. The number of comfortable and even elegant equipages here are altogether out of proportion with the amount of the population and their financial circumstances.

'Strange to say, however, all these brilliant equipages are quite an innovation in Madrid, and are due, I am told, to that suppression of convents and confiscation of Church property which seems here to have enriched everybody. People familiar with the place assure me that there was not one private carriage ten years ago where there are now 500, and hardly anything like a fine pair of horses in the whole town.

'The public promenade is a place of rest, and the afternoon the hour of recreation; morning and noon the rendezvous is at the Puerta del Sol, the chimney-corner and chaff-market of the Madrileños, where it is everybody's business to stand in everybody's way, where people push, and crowd, and swarm, as if only eager to rob each other of the sun's warmth, and to kill each other's time as well as their own.

'The Spaniard who can manage to get rid of his day between the Sun's-gate and the Castilian Fountain will be at no loss how to dispose of himself in the evening. The theatre will take off two or three of the dreariest hours, and at eleven, or soon afterwards, his club begins to brighten up. Whether it be for public amusements or for private entertainments, these Madrilenians are the most inveterate night-crows. The habit is, of course, contracted in the summer, when it is hardly possible to live except in the cool of the evening; but, whatever the time of the year may be, it is a fact that at their balls and *tertulias* people here begin to brighten up towards the small hours. Hardly any town in the world, Naples not excepted, seems to live more exclusively on amusement than " Royal Madrid." '

And so it seemed to us. We have wandered about the town from morning till night without seeing much sign of industry; and on the slightest pretext of a saint's day every shop is closed for some hours. There are numbers of Frenchmen now settled in Madrid, also Germans and Maltese who are the most industrious; but even they seem to make holiday two or three times a week. We have twice made our way into the little square (where birds and rabbits are sold) called the 'Plazuela Sta. Ana,' to M. Baillière's bookshop, and found it closed; and as he is a Frenchman, and this is almost the only place where foreign books can be bought, we hardly expected to find him keeping saints' days so rigidly.

But nothing is wonderful in Spain. The new café under the 'Grand Hôtel de Paris' is crowded day and night with people, some of whom look so poor and spend so little that it is a marvel to the uninitiated how they all live.

Our lasting impression of the people of Madrid will be, that one-third spent their lives in carriages, one-third in cafés, and one-third begged their bread.

The beggars are a great feature in all the streets, and pursue you with loud clamours for 'cuartos' in the name of 'our Lady of Atocha.'

They lounge about in groups in the most public places, and thrust themselves before you with an insolent, and sometimes threatening aspect, that does not by any means incite to charity. But then are they not licensed and numbered, and do they not beg 'officially' in the name of 'our holy mother the Church'?

In the interests of art, with which we have here most concern, we may hope that those picturesque groups of men, women, and children of all ages, that obstruct the entrance to every church, and stain the very doors with their filthy garments, may 'never cease out of the land;' but for the sake of true religion, and order, and public decency, we may ask the authorities at Madrid to protect strangers from annoyance and insult.

And the evil seems to grow: on the 1st January, 1866, we read that—

'The increase of mendicancy, and of all the outward evidence of real misery, in the streets of Madrid, have attained gigantic proportions, and people who have resided here for years aver that nothing like it has ever been witnessed within their recollection.'

In the present financial position of the country, it is doubtless difficult to grapple with such an amount of destitution and mendicancy, and even at all times to preserve public order; but we should have thought that the Church would be best consulting her own interest in not driving people from her doors. The theory is no doubt the same that holds in Rome, that the church steps and portals are the most fitting place for public charity, and that the hearts of worshippers are the most likely to expand with human pity; but they ride their hobby too hard in Spain, and, when strong and lusty men are seen crouching and shrinking in simulated pain (not one or two, but a dozen together), the natural impulse of most of us is to translate into pure Castilian those words that apply to one nation as well as to another:—'If a man will not work, neither shall he eat.'

Notwithstanding the evident poverty and distress which existed in Madrid when we were there, the dearness of provisions, and the poor quality of nearly everything exposed for sale in the markets, it is cheering to have another proof of the truth of the saying that there are 'two sides to every picture,' and to learn that, at the end of December, 1865, the Madrileños were not in the depths of despair:—

'In spite of all this distress, we have had a very merry Christmas here in the capital; flocks of fat turkeys gobbling about the streets for weeks; the Plaza Mayor, and its adjacent districts, one vast show of meat and vegetables, with great piles of grapes, pomegranates, and oranges, endless stalls of turrons, marzapanes, and other sweetmeats of the season, booths of children's toys, with all the paraphernalia of the Holy Manger, angels, shepherds, wise men, and "star in the East;" and all over town long strings of boys, as well as of grown-up men, with penny drums and farthing trumpets, keeping up a jolly noise for a day and a night, to the total murder of wholesome sleep.'

If our 'Lady Bountiful' smiles, all goes well: wherever be the secret springs—from whatever point the sun of prosperity shines—whether the good genius be a 'patron saint' of the Church, or a 'patron sinner,'[1] who holds for the time the keys of the public treasury, certain it is that at Christmas-time at Madrid, and during the 'Holy Week' at Seville, the tide of wealth flows—as we read that it flows in the 'oil cities' of the West.

If this is a puzzle to '*estranjeros*,' it is a perfect mystery to the more thoughtful of the inhabitants of Madrid, who feel certain, and do not hesitate to express their opinion, that a 'crash must come' some day, when the pay of the 'Guardias Civiles' will get too far into arrear,

---

[1] The misappropriation of public funds by Government officials has become so notorious, that we cannot use too strong an expression in alluding to it.

when the cry for bread will drown the noise of 'penny drums and farthing trumpets,' and we shall no longer read of 'three hundred Members of the Upper House, each driving to save his country in a coach and pair'!

CHAPTER V.

BULL-FIGHTS.

WE were sitting one evening in a crowded café near the Puerta del Sol, wondering, for want of something better to do, by what mysterious means such a magnificent establishment could manage to exist, when nearly every visitor contented himself with a glass of sugar and water, for which he paid a penny, and perhaps sat there the whole evening, smoking the '*cigaritos*' that he brought with him.

Flowers were brought to us for sale by most diminutive Señoritas; toys, books, songs, and newspapers, were handed about by itinerant vendors; and lottery tickets[1] with such 'excellent numbers' that we could have made 'a rapid fortune in a week if we had desired it—and *if* we were fortu-

---

[1] Lotteries are 'Cosas de España,' and are popular amongst all classes: there is a *Manual del Lotero* published at Madrid to guide the uninitiated. In our frontispiece Mr. Phillip has seized its more picturesque aspect, in a scene of everyday life in Spain.

nate.' We were listening to a monotonous song from a demonstrative young lady, in a rather short Andalusian costume, who accompanied herself on a guitar, and were becoming gradually confused with the noise of hundreds of voices and the fumes of cigarettes, when a group of men entered, on whom all eyes were instantly turned.

We heard the names of '*Cuchares*' and '*Dominguez*' whispered about, and soon learnt that these were the 'Espadas' and the performers who were to appear at the bull-fight the next day. They were fine, athletic, well-made men, with bright eyes and manly bearing; quiet in demeanour, and very neatly dressed in tight-fitting suits of black, with embroidered huzzar jackets and Spanish 'sombreros.' Their hair was cut closely, with the exception of one little plaited pigtail, which hung down at the back, just as the 'caballero' wears it, as shown in our frontispiece.

With them came in a crowd of young Madrileños, the sporting fraternity of Madrid, who discussed the chances of the morrow with much animation. The performers were by far the least excited of the group, and sat and sipped their coffee or '*agua*' with the greatest composure.

A Programme was produced, which we have printed on the next page.

PLAZA DE TOROS.

EN LA TARDE DEL LUNES 17 DE OCTUBRE DE 1864, SE VERIFICARÁ
(si el tiempo no lo impide)

LA 21.ª MEDIA CORRIDA DE TOROS.

PRESIDIRÁ LA PLAZA LA AUTORIDAD COMPETENTE.

Se lidiarán SEIS TOROS de las ganaderías y con las divisas siguientes:

TOROS.	GANADERIAS.	VECINDAD DEL GANADERO.	DIVISAS.
TRES	de D. Manuel Bañuelos y Salcedo.	Colmenar Viejo	Azul turquí
TRES	de D. Mauricio Rosendo	Madrid	Encarnada y amarilla.

LIDIADORES.

PICADORES.. *Francisco Calderon* y *Antonio Calderon*, con otros tres de reserva, sin que en el caso de inutilizarse los cinco pueda exigirse que salgan otros.

ESPADAS...... *Francisco Arjona Guillen* (Cúchares), *Gonzalo Mora* y *Antonio Carmona* (el Gordito), a cuyo cargo estarán las correspondientes cuadrillas de banderilleros, inclusa la del *Talo.*

SOBRESALIENTE DE ESPADAS, *Mariano Anton*, sin perjuicio de banderillear los toros que le correspondan.

El apartado de los toros se hará en la Plaza el dia de la corrida á las once y media. Los billetes para verle desde los balcones del corral y toriles, se espenderán á cuatro reales en la Administracion, contigua á las Caballerizas, desde las once en adelante.

LA CORRIDA EMPEZARÁ Á LAS
TRES Y MEDIA EN PUNTO.
Una música tocará antes de principiar la funcion y en los intermedios.

ESTADO para la corrida de Toros que ha de efectuarse en la tarde del LUNES 17 de Octubre de 1864.								
TOROS.	GANADERIAS.	PUYAZOS.	CAIDAS DE PICADORES.	CABALLOS.		PARES DE BANDERILLAS.	PASES DE MULETA.	ESTOCADAS - PINCHAZOS.
				MUERTOS.	HERIDOS.			
1.º....	Bañuelos.							
2.º....	Salcedo.							
3.º....	Bañuelos.							
4.º....	Salcedo.							
5.º....	Bañuelos.							
6.º....	Salcedo.							

This programme or play-bill gives the colours of the bulls, the names of their proprietors, and of the principal performers, &c. &c. The blank form on the back is intended to be filled up by the spectators with the feats of the 'Espadas,' 'Picadores,' &c., the number of horses killed, and other events, all of which are duly recorded in the newspapers.

Before we left the café we noticed the group in deep consultation with one Count ———, who it appeared had obtained permission to act as amateur 'Espada.' He was no novice, having a private bull-ring of his own.

On the following day we go early to obtain tickets, as it is supposed that some of the royal family will be present at the 'funcion,' and tickets are often difficult to procure in the afternoon. The office for their sale in the 'Calle de Alcalá' is a little wooden erection on the pavement, resembling those in the *Palais Royal* at Paris for the sale of newspapers.

The crowd, however, is here before us, in such numbers and apparently so eager that our expectation is raised to its highest pitch, and we feel the excitement to be catching. It is no orderly '*queue*' of people waiting two and two for their turn, as we are accustomed to see on the Continent, but a crushing, struggling, and surging mob, that sends up volumes of smoke, and ejaculations that are certainly not blessings. The majority fight their way to the 'despacho,' and fight their way back; then, buying a fan for one reale, and the little blue play-bill (that we have copied) for a cuarto, they disappear until the afternoon. The chief cause of all this disturbance is not the genuine eagerness of the crowd, but the system of speculators buying up tickets to sell again at exorbitant rates.

Whilst we are watching and making up our minds for a struggle, a tall, bright-eyed '*gamin*' comes up and offers his services.

'Shall he get a "carta" for us?'

'Yes, for the cheapest place on the *shady side* of the arena.'

In an instant he is plunging and crushing amongst the crowd, crawling over their heads; and, holding out our money with a long arm, he succeeds in getting one of the few remaining seats for two reales.

'But this "carta" is not marked "*al sombra*," and we cannot sit in the sun.'

'The Señor can have a fan for two reales, and it is the best side of the Plaza.'

The seats on the sunny side are about half the price of those marked '*al sombra*,' and the young gentleman, who kept a store of the former, had tried to foist one of them upon us, 'pocketing the difference.' Paper fans are sold for those who take these seats, but it is almost impossible to see when sitting facing the sun.

The performance commenced at three, and before two the whole population seemed to be moving towards the 'Plaza de Toros.'

> 'For once all men seemed one way drawn,
> Saw nothing else—heard nothing.'

Across the 'Puerta del Sol,' down the 'Calle de Alcala,' past the deserted 'Museo,' the almost as solitary 'Prado,' and through the 'Puerta de Alcala,' flowed the great river of men and women, gathering tributary streams at every street-corner, all eagerness and haste to see what they had seen a hundred times before.

There was one figure—and one only—in this crowd that told its purpose, and the sight was a sad one. A sorry steed, a veritable Rosinante, with gay tassels and trappings, was doing its best to prance and career up and down to attract the people, tottering under the weight of a lusty 'picador,' padded and covered with an armour of cork and leather to protect him from the bull's thrusts; followed by a boy on foot, whose office it would be to drive the poor beast when in the arena, and compel him to face the bull. The 'picador' rides gaily along, bowing to the people on each side, until they reach the entrance to the arena.

In every book that we ever read on Spain, it is stated that the best bull-fights are to be seen at Seville; but having seen them both at Madrid and Seville, we venture to think that this is no longer correct. 'Corridas de toros,' like everything else in Spain, have been affected by over-centralisation and railways; and the influx of strangers to Madrid has attracted the most distinguished 'Espadas' (with the fiercest bulls) to the capital, and caused more money to be spent upon performances here than in any part of Andalusia.

The 'Plaza de Toros' at Madrid is a low, ugly-looking building outside, with the general poor appearance of a second-rate circus, but with the addition of a peculiar and terrible smell as of shambles, that we do not forget to this day. The entrance to our seats was through a narrow passage behind some stables, where ten or twelve horses were eating their last meal of straw, and where harness and various 'properties' were piled up ready for use.

'On entering the ring,' says Mr. Ford, 'the stranger finds his watch put back at once eighteen hundred years; he is transported to Rome under the Cæsars; and, in truth, the sight is glorious of the assembled thousands in their Spanish costume: the novelty of the spectacle, associated with our earliest classical studies, is enhanced by the blue expanse of the heavens spread above as a canopy.'

We will endeavour to describe it as we found it. The interior of the building is in the form of a Roman amphitheatre, with a ring of about 1100 feet in circumference. Its general appearance is shabby and ruinous. Round the lower part, where we had taken places purposely, in order to get a good general view, there are ten rows of open seats rising one behind the other, with the number of inches allotted to each person painted upon them; behind are two tiers of shabby boxes, separated from us by a wooden railing, as a still further protection from the bulls. There is a royal box on the principal tier, and a few spacious ones on each side, decorated with tawdry hangings and devices, are reserved for the Court. We are separated from the ring by two wooden barriers about five and six feet high respectively, with an alley or passage between, which leads all round the ring, and serves as a place of refuge for the performers when hotly pursued, and for adventurous 'Madrileños' who wish to be near the scene of action. Opposite the royal box are the doors where the bulls enter, and at the sides two others for the performers. The seats about us and the benches above are worn and weather-beaten, and there seems to have been little attempt made to repair or redecorate the building.

There is, as has been truly said, a 'business-like and murderous look about the whole building' which is unmistakable. When we entered, the centre of the ring was as crowded with people as the course at Epsom on the Derby day before the great race. At the sound of a trumpet the ring was gradually cleared, and we soon found ourselves tightly wedged up on all sides, beyond all possibility of retreat if we had desired it. In front, leaning on the ropes, were young men and boys armed with sticks and fireworks, ready to take part in the performance if they could get a chance, which they occasionally managed to do.

The crowd was not demonstrative or very noisy; it was, on the whole, a goodhumoured holiday mob, which seemed to care more for a '*cigarito*' than anything else in the world; but there were a few *connoisseurs* near us and round the bull-contractor's box who were discussing the chances of the day, and might have been betting, but that there is so little real speculation or 'sporting' amongst Spaniards. The excitement of real danger to the performers, and curiosity as to how each bull will behave, seem to be the paramount attractions.

We said that the crowd was not noisy, but, when the seats were nearly full, the sound that went up from more than eight thousand people was deafening; and the smoking was a wonderful sight, resembling an enormous circle of burning peat, or the smouldering of camp fires. Almost the only distinguishable sounds were the incessant scratching of fusees or matches, and the cry everywhere for water—*Agua! agua! agua!* The water-carriers were in constant requisition all through the performance, for the heat was very great.

The majority of the people were dressed in Spanish costume, and were evidently from the country and suburbs of Madrid. All true Madrileños of course wore black coats and Paris hats, but the ladies in the boxes, of whom there were a number, generally had fans and wore the mantilla.

Just before the commencement of the performance the sun shone out brilliantly, and in an instant a thousand paper fans of all colours fluttered in the breeze, looking in the distance as if a swarm of butterflies had suddenly started into life.

Another signal from the trumpeter: the band played, and from a general movement in the crowd we knew that the royal box had its occupant (although we could see no one), and that the signal to commence had been given.

A side-door is opened, and the combatants enter in procession, led by two mounted officers of police in ancient Spanish costume, with black hats and cloaks. The procession itself, and the whole effect when the spectators rise to see the entry, is so imposing and unique, that we should recommend every one to see this, if not to stay for the fight. After the '*alguaciles*' or officers come the '*picadores*,' mounted on their poor steeds and armed to the teeth, holding heavy lances in their hands; after them the '*banderillos*' and '*chulos*,' or combatants on foot, fine, active men, in the costume we are accustomed to see in the opera of 'Figaro' or 'The Barber of Seville.' Next follow the '*matadores*' (or '*espadas*,' as they are generally called), the '*maestros*,' whose office it is to kill the bull single-handed. Lastly, come a number of attendants, and a team of mules three abreast gaily caparisoned, which are afterwards employed to drag away the dead.

The performers bow before the royal box, and a key of the door by which the bulls are to enter is thrown to them by the president. All then retire from the ring excepting two 'picadores' on horseback; the trumpet sounds again, and the door is thrown open.

This is the supreme moment; every eye and ear is on the stretch, and there is a general hush throughout the crowd. A low roaring is heard in the dark passage leading from the dens, and in a few seconds, with a plunging, awkward motion, the bull rushes into the centre of the ring and stands still; dazzled apparently with the brightness and sudden change from his dark prison, and startled with the shout that greets his entry. The first bull on this day was a handsome black beast, rather small, of Andalusian breed, with enormous horns, and apparently of great strength and activity. His coat was glossy and bright, and was decorated with ribbons of the colour of his owner (*azul turqui*), pinned on to his shoulder.

His first impulse seemed to be to find his way out of all this uproar, and get back to his den;

but all such thoughts evidently vanished when he caught sight of the 'picadores' drawn up near the barrier one on each side of the ring. He faced about at once, and with a motion, well described ' as though body and legs were borne helplessly along by the enormous throat, which, working in every muscle, seemed to sway itself over the earth by its own mere weight,' he rushed headlong at man and horse and threw them both to the ground with a crash. Instantly the 'chulos' and 'banderillos' entered the ring, and with their bright red flags drew away the bull from the fallen picador. Then commenced a chase and a series of passages and rushes, in which the chulos displayed marvellous dexterity in evading the bull, sometimes waiting for his approach, and, just as the animal stooped to toss them, *stepping on its forehead*, walking along its back, and jumping easily off again. Sometimes they were so hotly pursued that they had to drop their flags and leap the barriers.[1]

In the mean time the 'picador' had been dragged from under his wounded horse and remounted, and the ring was again cleared of every

---

[1] At the Plaza at Seville there are screens for the performers to run behind, but at Madrid there is no escape but by leaping the barriers.

one on foot. The same scene occurred with slight variations; the more skilful 'picadores' managed sometimes to receive the charge of the bull with their lances and to drive him back; but, in the end, the horses were fearfully wounded, and often fell dead under their riders. The 'picadores' appeared much shaken by the falls, and it looked dangerous work, but we heard that they were seldom seriously injured. After several horses had been killed,[1] the 'picadores' retired, and the more skilful and graceful part of the performance commenced.

The trumpet sounded again, and the 'banderillos,' advancing with two little barbed darts about a foot long, entered the ring, and, standing upright with their arms raised above their heads, received the charge of the bull, jumping aside and endeavouring at that instant to fix the darts on his shoulder—an operation which, as our neighbour informed us, 'should be done neatly—one on each side.' This of course enrages the bull, and renders the sport most exciting to those who love it.

He roared and tore up the earth with rage, and rushed headlong after his tormentors, who

---

[1] On this day we saw eight horses lying dead or dying in the ring at one time, and one picador carried out insensible.

had 'hairbreadth' escapes, jumping the barriers when the bull was almost upon them. They immediately returned to the charge, and darted about the arena, waving their cloaks in the bull's face, and tormenting him until his rage was terrible to behold.

The excitement at this time was at its highest pitch, and to enter the ring at all seemed, to novices, most dangerous. Two 'banderillos' advanced cautiously, holding their darts high in the air. They stood too close to each other, and when the bull rushed at them one tripped against the other and fell down. In an instant the ring was filled with 'chulos' to the rescue, who, in their turn, were scattered right and left; several ran for the barrier within a few yards of us, and the bull followed them closely.

We saw him coming plunging towards us; and although several women shrieked and people jumped from their seats, we did not at the moment apprehend danger. Surely, we thought (if there was time to think), it is so arranged that the bull cannot leap *both* barriers and reach the seats. But this was one of the '*cosas de España*' that we had yet to learn; we did not know that this was a favourite part of the performance, and the 'fun' that all those young gentlemen with red handkerchiefs and sticks like Smithfield cattle-drovers had come out to see.

The bull tried to leap the barrier, and failed; he turned away with a sullen roar, and ploughed up the earth about him. The 'banderillos' and 'chulos' returned again to the ring, but he was either craven or obstinate, or (as we thought) out of breath, and fairly beaten; nothing would stir him.

Then the monotonous cry, that we had heard incessantly throughout the fight, of '*Agua!*' '*agua!*' was changed to another cry—for 'fire.' '*Fuega!*' '*fuega!*' '*fuega!*' was echoed round the ring, and in answer to the call a 'banderillo' advanced with two darts, shaped like the others, but covered with white paper. He stealthily approached the bull, who stood motionless in the middle of the ring, and, skilfully planting the darts on the bull's shoulder, beat a rapid retreat. The darts were loaded with hand-rockets, and immediately exploded on his back. He turned round and leaped into the air in terror and pain, while the people rose and screamed with excitement. Suddenly seeing his tormentor leaning over the barrier, he made after him, and, getting his fore-feet and head on to the wood-work, he fairly toppled over and fell into the passage between the two partitions. Here he was immediately set upon by the young gentlemen, who with their sticks tried to drive him back. He turned upon them, however, and cleared the *second* barrier, how we know not, and, sooner than we can write it, was amongst us, and walking up the seats within three feet of where we sat. The proverb that 'he who hesitates is lost' was never better illustrated. To hesitate, to run away, or to make room for the bull, would have been fatal; the plan adopted instantly by all was to fasten upon him in a body, man, woman, or child, whoever was nearest, and so by sheer dead weight of numbers *walk him back* into the ring!

And now the third act commenced, the ring was cleared, and one of the 'espadas' entered alone. He was dressed as daintily as if he were going to a ball, with an embroidered suit of gay colours, and silk stockings, exactly as we see him in our illustration. He threw his cap to the ground, and, with his sword in his right hand, and a '*muleta*' or red flag in his left, advanced to meet the bull, amidst the cheers of the people.

It was an exciting moment for any one to see, for the first time, this man standing alone before the bull, his life depending upon his quickness of

eye and his trusty sword, and with his fine figure (clad with almost effeminate delicacy and grace), separated not three feet from his enraged antagonist. The bull at first seemed to hesitate, but soon made a rush at the 'espada,' who skilfully turned it off by waving the muleta and jumping aside. This was repeated a dozen or twenty times, during which the bull was slightly wounded, but, suddenly choosing his opportunity, when the bull had lowered his head to the right position, the 'espada' pointed his sword steadily at a spot between the horns, and the bull ran upon it and *killed himself*,—falling dead at one blow. This was applauded vehemently, and caps were thrown by the spectators into the ring, which the performer had the trouble of throwing back again to the owners—a peculiar form of compliment which every one seemed to appreciate.

Immediately the gates were thrown open, and the mules were brought in to take away the dead; they were splendid animals, and galloped off rapidly with the bull and the dead horses, and in five minutes the ring was cleared and another victim rushed in. The second bull was a poor-looking animal—tame and frightened, that ran away from the 'picadores,' and tried to escape out of the ring. However, after a time, he turned upon his tormentors, and the same performances were gone through as before, but with less spirit. The only event of importance was the entry of the amateur 'espada,' whom we had seen in the café the previous evening. He was greatly cheered by the people, and showed plenty of courage and self-possession: but it was a wretched blundering business, wounding the bull cruelly with false thrusts, and failing to kill him in the required time. The poor beast had to be put out of his misery by a professional executioner.

This was enough; we had done our duty, and had seen a Spanish bull-fight as it is conducted in the year 1864. Perhaps we wish never to see another: we say 'perhaps' because we fear that there were one or two moments during the fight that we would willingly live over again if we had the chance.

Do away with horses altogether (as in Mexico), divest the exhibition of all unnecessary cruelty, give the animal fair play, and a bull-fight has in it the elements of true sport, which are irresistible to an Englishman.

Such an exhibition of skill and daring as we saw that day will not be soon forgotten; and we are bound to confess we enjoyed, what our better nature condemned; agreeing with the late Richard Cobden that 'so long as this continues to be the popular sport of high and low, so long will Spaniards be indifferent to human life, and have their civil contests marked with displays of cruelty which make men shudder.'

CHAPTER VI.

MADRID — PICTURE GALLERIES — ROYAL PALACE, &c.

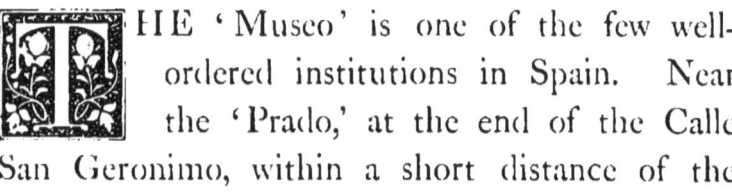

THE 'Museo' is one of the few well-ordered institutions in Spain. Near the 'Prado,' at the end of the Calle San Geronimo, within a short distance of the centre of the city, open at convenient hours nearly every day, with civil and obliging attendants, and every facility afforded to view the pictures, no wonder that to strangers and all lovers of art this should be the favourite spot in Madrid; but curiously enough, it is the one place where a Spaniard is hardly ever seen.

In this world-famous collection there are, according to the catalogue which we purchase at the doors, forty-six paintings by Murillo, ten Raphaels, sixty-two Rubens, fifty-three Teniers, sixty-four Velasquez, twenty-two Van Dycks, forty-three Titians, twenty-five Veroneses, thirty-four Tintorettos, besides numerous works by Breughel,

Bassano, Snyder, Poussin, Wouvermans, Ribera, Luca Giordano, Guido, and Claude. The rooms are large and well lighted, but there are hardly any seats for visitors. The paintings are well hung, clearly numbered, and easily referred to in the catalogue.

In the Rotunda, near the entrance, the paintings are generally inferior, and the room on our right hand, devoted to '*las escuelas contemporaneos*' (the modern school), will not detain us long.

In the central hall and in the 'Salon de Isabel' are some of the best pictures, but the general arrangement and classification enable the visitor to study the works of each master separately. Murillo is seen to better advantage at Seville, his native place; but we have here the celebrated picture of the '*Immaculate Conception*,' which, by some, is considered finer than his painting of the same subject in the Gallery of the Louvre at Paris; The '*Holy Family;*' The '*Annunciation;*' The '*Vision of St. Bernard;*' '*Agnus Dei;*' '*Mater Dolorosa*,' &c.; and the picture, so often copied, of The '*Infant Saviour giving St. John to drink out of a shell.*'

Most of his works seem to have been retouched in parts, and sometimes even repainted; so that this part of the collection is rather disappointing. What struck us most was the apparent want of tone and h⸺ ·y of colour, and of that marvellous 'quality with which we are familiar in England, in the comparatively few examples we possess at the Dulwich Galle⸺ elsewhere.

But Mr. Ford will assist us to explain thi⸺

'On Murillo,' he writes, ⸺ ous experiments have been tried by the o⸺ ,ers, poulticers, and plasterers. However, he is so ⸺ ⸺ ⸺ ct, so dramatic, comes so home to, and appeal⸺ ⸺ to the common sense of mankind, and is recommended by such a magical fascination of colour, that he capti⸺ alik⸺ the learned and unlearned. He has far more g⸺ ice⸺ but far ⸺ of the masculine mind, than Velasquez, wh⸺ co⸺ d to him, seems somewhat cold and grey in colour; for Murillo painted flesh as he saw it in Andalusia, roasted, toasted, and bronzed by the glowing sun, and not recalling the pale unripened beauty of the north. Like Titian his strength lay in ravishing *colour*; none ever rivalled him in the luminous diaphanous streams of golden ether in which his cherubs float like butterflies. . . . Murillo, like Velasquez, lacked the highest quality of the Italian ideal; true Spaniards, they were local, and imitated nature as they saw her; thus Murillo's holy subjects are not glorified forms and visions which compel us to bow knee and adore, but pleasing scenes of a domestic ⸺ ⸺here sports of graceful children attract the delighted a⸺ of affectionate parents. There is neither the awful sublimity ⸺ ⸺hael Angelo, nor the unearthly purity of Raphael.'

In the presence of so m⸺ al grace and beauty, and in contemplation ⸺ imaginative power displayed in some of these works, perhaps we shall hardly agree in the whole of the above, but will reserve our judgment of this master until we see him at Seville.

If the collection of Murillos is incomplete, we are able to appreciate the full power and humour of VELASQUEZ; his power, in nearly every picture by his hand, but notably in '*Don Baltasar on Horseback*' (No. 332), young Prince Carlos on a pony, represented riding at full gallop towards the spectator; and his humour in No. 138 (*Los Borrachos*), and in the two figures of *Mænipo* and *Æsop*, Nos. 245 and 254. One of his most important works is the '*Surrender of Breda*' (No. 319), which has been described as 'perhaps the finest picture of Velasquez; never were knights, soldiers, or national character better painted, or the heavy Fleming, the intellectual Italian, and the proud Spaniard, more nicely marked, even to their boots and breeches: the lances of the guards actually vibrate.'

Number 155 is a curious picture, representing the artist painting the portrait of the *Infanta Margarita*, daughter of Philip IV. She is attended by her dwarfs, and in the background are seen Philip IV. and his queen. The execution of this picture, in which every figure is a portrait, is most careful in details, and in the rendering of costume. The dwarfs that he introduces here are reproduced in other pictures with an almost painful lifelike effect, and indeed every historical figure painted by him bears evidence of truth. His picture of Philip IV. (No. 299) was used as a model for the bronze statue of that monarch in the 'Plaza del Oriente.'

But Velasquez, like other figure-painters of our own time and nation, believed that his forte lay in landscape, and nothing pleased him better than to follow the court to the *Versailles* of Madrid and pourtray the glories of the gardens at Aranjuez: No. 145 is a good illustration of this class of subject.

There are examples of other Spanish painters that we cannot detail, some of which are only to be found after repeated visits to the 'Museo,' and by confining ourselves religiously to one school at a time. Nearly every visitor passes from the works of Murillo and Velasquez to those of Raphael, Titian, Rembrandt, Guido, Paul Veronese, Rubens, Van Dyck, Poussin, Claude de Lorraine, Albert Durer, Holbein, &c., neglecting, or scarcely giving sufficient attention to, those of Ribera, Zurbaran, and others, who especially illustrate Spanish painting and Spanish life.

The Madrid gallery is by no means complete, and, like everything else in Spain, is a 'creature of accident,' a collection of about two thousand pictures got together by chance, and preserved by Spaniards for the benefit of strangers.

The sculpture and antiquities collected here are not remarkable, but there are several rooms devoted to them, through which the visitor is conducted at certain intervals during the day. There are also some curious and costly inlaid mosaic tables.

A good descriptive account of the whole collection (as now arranged) has, we believe, yet to be written. Nearly every Englishman that has visited these galleries has examined them by the light of Ford, whose terse and vigorous language, power of description, and undeniable authority on all things Spanish, have made him a 'cicerone' as fascinating as irresistible. But his account of the pictures in the Museo was written more than twenty years ago: there have been many changes and additions to the gallery since that time, and our knowledge of the works of the old masters, and our estimate of them, has also changed considerably.

At a time when so many of our countrymen

are flocking to Madrid for the purpose of seeing the 'Museo,' such a description as we have hinted at would be valuable.[1]

At the opposite end of Madrid (near the 'Plaza del Oriente,' and the statue of Philip IV.) stands the Royal Palace. It is the 'emphatic feature' of the city, and is almost the only building which dwells in the recollection of the visitor. Situated in a commanding position above the river Manzanares, with a fine view of the Guadarama mountains from its north front, it occupies the best and most prominent position in Madrid; and in keeping with everything royal in Spain, it is on a magnificent scale, having cost upwards of 800,000*l.*

'It forms,' says Mr. O'Shea, 'a square of 471 feet, is 100 feet high, and belongs to the Tuscan style; the base is granite, and the upper portion is built of the beautiful white stone of Colmenar, which resembles marble. In the centre is a "patio" 140 feet square. The interior arrangements are also magnificent.'

When the Queen is absent most of the apart-

---

[1] Students will do well to obtain Mr. O'Neil's Lectures delivered at the Royal Academy in the present year, and just announced for publication.

ments may be seen, also the *Chapel Royal* and the *Stables* and *Coach-houses;* these last contain a curious collection of vehicles, upwards of one hundred in number, built at different periods. In the royal stables there are a number of Arab horses, ponies, and mules, of the finest breeds, and the liveries, harness, and trappings are well worth seeing.

The *Armoury*, which is in a building near the Palace, is said to be one of the best collections in Europe, where there are not only a number of historically interesting objects, but also some of the finest and most unique designs for helmets, shields, &c.

The *Royal Library* should be examined; it contains upwards of 250,000 volumes, and a collection of coins. It is, we read,

'very rich in works of Spanish literature, but the catalogue is not well classified, and a new one lately begun is not likely to be finished for a long time. The officials are civil, but know little about the contents, and Mr. Panizzi would be invaluable here. There is a fine collection of coins and medals, numbering upwards of 150,000, which was begun with the celebrated numismatic collection of the Abbé Rothlen of Orleans. They were very well classified, and are most interesting as illustrating the early history of Roman, Gothic, and Moorish Spain.'

There was great discussion amongst the visitors

as to the merits of this much boasted collection of coins, some of the most learned maintaining that it is neither as authentic or complete as would appear from the catalogue. On this point we will not venture an opinion, but would suggest to those who take most interest in such matters that there is a perfect mine of wealth in manuscripts and books and coins stored up (for they are never used) both at Madrid and at the 'Escorial.' Strangers are permitted to examine almost everything in these buildings at certain times, but under strict *surveillance*. The glass cases and padlocked chests with their precious contents sometimes require a 'silver key' to open them; but much can be done for a 'peseta.'

One day had to be devoted to a hurried visit to the 'Escorial,' the Tomb of the Spanish Kings, that strange, desolate-looking pile that we passed by railway on coming to Madrid, standing almost alone, at an elevation of 2700 feet above the sea, in the midst of a wilderness of stones, from which it has been constructed. It is a building of enormous extent, of the 'Doric' order, with four towers at the corners, and a central dome.[1]

[1] For its history, and detailed description of its chapels, sacristy, oratorios, library, &c., see O'Shea's 'Guide to Spain.' p 127.

To see the Escorial is a hard day's work. After two hours' journey by railway, it takes the visitor five hours merely to go over the building with a guide, which will give some idea of its extent. This is the routine, which it is difficult to break through, or to obtain anything like a quiet view of this wonderful place.

After the Escorial there seemed little to detain us at Madrid. We went of course to pay our devotions at the shrine of the 'Lady of Atocha,' and to see other notable churches; but our spirits soon flagged, and we could not get up an interest in any of them. We began to long for the 'sunny South,' to get away from the noise and rabble of Madrid, and, in truth, to get out of the wind. Until we had felt the warm breath of Andalusia; until we had heard the songs of the 'dark-eyed daughters of Cadiz;' seen *Sevilla la* '*maravilla*,' and visited the 'last home of the banished Moor' at Granada, we had not seen Spain.

But how to get there? Travellers who will (we trust in this very year 1866) be able to go easily by railway from Madrid to Seville or Granada without any more trouble than they would experience in going from London to

Edinburgh, would hardly believe the difficulties that stood in our way. In the winter of 1864 it was impossible to reach even Cordova without travelling incessantly for two nights and a day, and passing twenty-four, or sometimes thirty, hours in a diligence. The fares were enormous (varying every day according to the demand), and no places in the diligence could be secured without giving some days' notice. The train for the south left Madrid every night, and only went to Santa Cruz, near the Sierra Morena.

Our last two days in the capital were entirely taken up with preparations for the departure, the chief part of the time being occupied in endeavouring to obtain sufficient money (in gold and silver) from our bankers in exchange for letters of credit. It was with the greatest difficulty that our party could get together fifty pounds after giving two or three days' notice. There was plenty of 'paper' of the Bank of Spain; but we should have lost greatly by taking it, and it would not pass in the South.

Money matters had not improved in December, 1865, when the following paragraph appeared in the newspapers:—

'*Madrid, Dec.* 12.—To conceive an idea of the state of monetary affairs in this country, it will be sufficient to glance at some of the transactions of the National Bank. There is here a " Bank of Spain," whose notes are of no use whatever outside the gates of Madrid. These notes are not taken at the various metropolitan railway stations; at least the ticket-office plainly refuses to give any change due on them. The money-exchangers only give change for them at 2 per cent. discount, and shop and innkeepers, as a matter of course, " consider " the discount in their bills. The Bank professes to be ready to cash the notes at sight; but as they have only one cashier at work, and the payments are limited to 40*l.* worth at a time, the cash-office is beset by the agents of the money-changers waiting for their turn *en queue,* crowding, pushing, and storming, with such violence as often leads to quarrels of the most serious character.'

Several hours were also spent in that most wretched institution the '*Correo*,' or General Post Office, in the vain endeavour to decipher the names on the lists (which are copied out and hung up) of letters directed ' *Poste Restante.*' As Sir John ——'s name was put amongst the s's, and Henry B——'s amongst the h's, and as nearly all the addresses were illegible, it was a weary work of time to find them out in a dark, crowded room. The entrance to the '*Correo*' in a narrow court behind the 'Puerta del Sol,' and the dirty staircase by which every one has to approach this little dungeon, will be fresh in the memory of many of our countrymen, as the Post Office is generally the first and last place they visit in Madrid.

Before leaving finally for the South we went to Toledo, which we must describe in the next chapter.

CHAPTER VII.

MADRID — ARANJUEZ — TOLEDO.

WE leave Madrid by the Alicante and Valencia Railway, and pass through a poor and uncultivated district, which begins to improve and show signs of life when, in about two hours, we arrive at ARANJUEZ, the 'Spanish Fontainebleau' as it has been called, but which is hardly worthy of its name. It is here that the Court resides for a few weeks during the hot season, seeking the cool shade of trees and clustering vines that luxuriate by the banks of the Tagus. This was almost the first green and cultivated spot that we had seen since we left the Pyrenees, and poor as it was, flat and formal (and to English eyes rather dreary), the change from the treeless windy Sierras was most grateful.

The Palace is built in the Louis XIV. style, with hardly anything Spanish about it, and the town is formed of long, straight streets, of poorly-built houses, more formal and monotonous, and wanting in colour, than anything we meet with, even in France.

There is little to repay a visitor for wandering through the rooms of the Palace, which are visible when the Court is absent; the paintings, chiefly by Spanish artists, are poor, but there is a Titian in the chapel, and a Teniers in one of the Queen's apartments. Lovers of *bijouterie* and articles of *vertù* will find some curious and costly examples of inlaying in ebony, ivory, and metals, in the smaller rooms, which may be seen for a small fee.

But we took more interest in the gardens, in wandering about under the shade of grand old elms and cedars of Lebanon, and in examining the ruins of fountains and sculpture that are scattered over the grounds. In the Museo at Madrid we have seen in a painting by Velasquez what these gardens once were, and the costumes of the Court in the time of Philip II. A poor imitation of Fontainebleau one would think at the best: now, after having passed through various changes of resuscitation and neglect, their last state is not much better than a weedy wilderness of walks and straggling flower-beds, laid out in that formal style which is nothing if not neat and prim.

Nevertheless there are green pastures seen through the trees, cattle feeding, and pleasant signs of cultivation.

It is here that we first realize the fact that Spain has rivers. We are standing on the banks of the Tagus, that 'mighty river' 375 miles long, which takes its rise far away eastward amongst the rocky mountains above Cuenca; as Ford describes it:

'Winding its most poetical and picturesque course to Lisbon—first green and arrowy amid the yellow cornfields of new Castile; then freshening the sweet "Tempe" of Aranjuez, clothing the gardens with verdure, and filling the nightingale-tenanted glens with groves; then boiling and rushing around the granite ravines of rock-built Toledo, hurrying to escape from the cold shadows of its deep prison, and dashing joyously into light and liberty, to wander far away into silent plains, and on to Talavera, where its waters were dyed with brave blood. Triumphantly it rolls thence under the shattered arches of Almaraz, down to desolate Estremadura, in a stream as tranquil as the azure sky by which it is curtained, yet powerful enough to force the mountains at Alcantara.

'How stern, solemn, and strikingis this Tagus of Spain! no commerce has ever made it its highway—no English steamer has ever civilised its waters. Its rocks have witnessed battles, not peace; have reflected castles and dungeons, not quays or warehouses; few cities have risen on its banks: it is truly a river of Spain—that isolated and solitary land!'

We have gone half through Spain, and have seen hardly any rivers. We crossed streams and torrents coming over the Pyrenees: there was the little river Arlanzon at Burgos, and the dry bed of the Manzanares at Madrid, but these were nearly all.

There are, as may be seen on our map, five principal rivers, which have their sources in the mountains and high table-lands of Spain. The *Tagus*, of which we have just spoken; the *Guadalquivir* in Andalusia, which we shall see at Seville and Cadiz, and which is navigable between those two places; the *Guadiana*, running through the low plains of Estremadura on the south-west; the *Ebro*, 450 miles long, which completely crosses the north of Spain, its sources in the mountains near Bilbao, its outlet into the Mediterranean near Lerida in the east, and on which the cities of Tudela and Saragossa are built; and the *Douro*, which we crossed at Valladolid, and which runs into the Atlantic at Oporto.

Besides these there are numerous smaller streams, many of which are dry in the summer, and in the rainy season overflow their banks. In the plains, the country is often flooded for miles, and in the mountainous districts the swollen rivers do scarcely less damage, by carrying away bridges and dwellings in their downward course to the sea. Some have forced themselves altogether into new channels, and it is not uncommon to have to ford a river or cross by a ferry-boat within sight of a massive Roman bridge, which is standing high and dry on the bank. If some one would only come and rebuild them over the errant rivers, it would be a great boon to the country; but it is quite certain that the Spaniards will never do it for themselves.

This supineness, or whatever it may be called, this neglect of both roads and rivers, is the great secret of the ill success of Spanish railroads, because the communication between the towns and the stations is always bad, and there is no attempt at improvement. French speculators will have to depend upon what is called 'through traffic' to the great towns, and must make their own roads as well as railways (as is being done at Toledo) if they ever hope for a dividend.

Aranjuez is about twenty-five miles from Toledo; the journey takes an hour and a half by railway; and there are several trains during the day. The terminus at Toledo is outside the town, near the bridge of Alcantara. A good broad road is in course of construction, which will make the approach to the town comparatively easy to future travellers; but in 1864 our rickety omnibus was dragged by a number of mules up streets which were more like flights of stairs with the steps loose, than any passage fit for a vehicle. The fact is, that no one should attempt to ride in Toledo excepting on a mule; but the railway was an innovation, which brought another in the shape of an omnibus, and travellers have to take the consequences.

Our illustration will give some idea of the general position and aspect of Toledo, which is built on a great rock and has two walls; the inner built, it is said, in the seventh century, the outer by Alonso VI. in 1109. The walls were destroyed in many places when the town was bombarded by the French, and the 'débris' looks as if it had been left untouched since that time. You can actually see where a building or a wall was undermined or destroyed, by the stones that still lie in heaps everywhere. It is more like a city of the dead than the living; the rocks seem burnt and charred, as if they would crumble at a touch. In the summer the heat is intense; there is no shade excepting in the narrow streets, and the Tagus then becomes a 'poor, muddy, sluggish stream.'

Standing upon the ramparts above the town, and looking down upon its narrow streets and ruined buildings, we can point out at once the

remains of Moorish refinement and taste in the construction of their dwellings, and cannot help longing for a glimpse of the city when the Moors held possession.

The Moorish buildings of Toledo, clustering together round the mountain-side, nestling as it were into the crevices of the great rock upon which the city stands, contrasted with the more modern *Alcazar*, and other buildings of a still later period, were the first striking instances of that want of harmony between the two leading styles of architecture in Spain that we afterwards found so common in the South.

The '*Gate of the Sun*,' with its pointed horse-shoe arch and massive turrets, which has since been restored and propped up by Castilians, preserves enough of its ancient character for us to understand what it once was, and presents at the present time an excellent subject for the artist's pencil.

But we shall better appreciate the buildings in Toledo if we glance for a moment at the general character of the architecture in Spain, passing over the period of occupation by the Romans, the Goths, and other nations, that by turns held possession of the country, and speaking only of the last seven hundred years—the period when the finest cathedrals in Spain were built.

In the north, at Burgos, Leon, Segovia, Valladolid, and Toledo, we find, perhaps, the best examples of 'pointed Gothic' in the world. In the south, the Moors, who overran Spain during all this period, built the great mosque at Cordova; the *Alcazar* and *Giralda* at Seville; and the *Alhambra* at Granada.

Mr. Street says that, 'from the first invasion by the Moors in 711, down to their expulsion from Granada in 1492, their whole history was mixed up with that of the Christians, and, as might be expected, so great was the detestation in which the two races held each other, that neither of them borrowed to any great extent from the art of the other, and accordingly we see two streams of art flowing as it were side by side, a circumstance almost, if not quite, unknown at the same period in any other part of Europe.'

Passing from the north to the south of Spain in the direction shown on the map, the contrast between the styles is very striking, but it harmonizes with the equally striking change in the aspect of the country. Thus in Castile, that dry and sterile land, cold, passionless, cheerless, barren—by what accident, sympathy, or law of life, we know not—Gothic architects rear their proudest monuments. Passing southwards into Andalusia—a land of olives, palms, orange-groves, and sunny watered plains—the cathedral is a mosque, and there is hardly an example of early Gothic to be found.

The contrast is suggestive of more than we can here give space for: our 'cicerone' is waiting at the street-corner to take us over the city.

Winding our way through the maze of narrow lanes or streets, so narrow that we can touch both sides at once, we pass many deserted Moorish dwellings, some with the outer doors still remaining, studded with enormous nails and knockers, just as they had been left centuries ago. The houses are nearly all built on the same plan, with neatly-tiled passages leading from the street into a central courtyard or patio, with a gallery all round, on to which all the upper rooms open. The galleries are of wood, with carved lattice-work, in a tolerable state of preservation, and the walls not unfrequently bear traces of Moresque decoration. Some of these buildings are used as warehouses and carpenters' shops, some are entirely deserted, but you may still find pieces of exquisite work amongst the rubbish-heaps which abound.

The remains of wells, which once occupied the centre of the courtyards, are sometimes to be met with. One we noticed, in a good state of preservation, had been beautifully carved; the marble round the top was polished, and worn into deep vandykes by the action of the rope. In some of the most important of the ruins there are traces of the original colours used in decorating the walls and ceilings.

Mr. Street says that one of the best examples of Moorish buildings is to be found 'in a room in a garden behind the house No. 6 in the *Calle de Plata*,' and there is another on a larger scale in the '*Casa de Mesa*,' which the guides will point out. Although not apparently an enthusiastic admirer of Moorish work,[1] he bears ready testimony to their grace and beauty as seen here in ruin.

'Of these,' he says, 'the most remarkable that I have seen are in that interesting city of Toledo, which, so far as I can learn, seems to surpass Seville in work of this kind almost as much as it does in its treasures of Christian art.

'Here it is plain that, *whilst Christians ruled the city, Moors inhabited it.* The very planning of the town, with its long, narrow, winding lanes; the arrangement of the houses,

---

[1] Probably from the *surface* character of all Moorish decoration; but he remarks, 'They deserve a detailed notice, because they prove, as do most of their works, that plaster may be used truthfully and artistically, and that, without any approach to the contemptible effect which the imbecility and dishonesty of the nineteenth-century designers of plaster-work have contrived to impress on almost all their productions.'

with their closed outer walls, their patios or courts, and their large and magnificent halls, speak strongly and decidedly in favour of the Moorish origin of the whole; and when we come to look into the matter in detail, this presumption is most fully supported; for everywhere the design of the internal finishing and decorations of the houses and rooms is thoroughly Moorish, executed with the remarkable skill in plaster for which the Moors were noted.'

Nothing in the architectural history of any nation is more remarkable than the orthodox spirit in which the Moors worked, scarcely showing any sign of contact with other nations, or even a trace of the influence of Christian art, in any of their buildings; preserving to the last their distinctive character, their refinement and exquisite taste.

These are the houses to which the banished Moor looks forward to return, and the keys of which he still so carefully preserves. We have seen them hanging up in Moorish houses in Algiers,[1] but never realized until now their true purpose.

---

[1] 'The Moors have a fixed idea that they will some day recover their property in Spain, and still preserve with care the keys of their old homes. They have waited for centuries, and still wait; it may be for some kingly summons from the walls of the Alhambra, or the gardens of the Generaliffe. But the long-expected messenger makes no sign; the Moors and their Spanish paradise are yet divided. Years pass on, the pattern of the key is now of a past age, and the Mediterranean rolls between them still!'—*Life in Algeria.*

There were some amongst our party who discussed, as we rambled over the town, the possibility, to use no stronger word, of time bringing this to pass; and perhaps the chances of such a change are not as remote as might appear at first sight. Instead of advancing in civilization with other nations, Spain is standing still;[1] which is only another word for retrogression. Wherever we go we see the same signs and hear the same story. Spain will not help herself, and is almost bankrupt. What nation will step forward to redeem her? What nation may not be tempted to try to reconquer her?

Many such thoughts crowd upon us whilst wandering about this noble and desolate city, once the capital and pride of Spain, now a rock covered with ruins. 'Upstart Madrid' is a poor apology for what this city must once have been, but it is only another sign of the instability and indifference which we mark everywhere.

There is little of the bustle and business of life apparent, even in the more central parts of Toledo; and in the *Tocodover*, or Moorish square, formerly the mart for commerce from all parts of the world, there are only a few shops

---

[1] Excepting where foreign nations have taken the initiative, and compelled her to advance with the age.

open. The greatest stir is occasioned by the daily sight-seers from Madrid, who crowd the little extortionate *Fonda de Lino*, and attract a crowd of idlers and beggars all day.

We may explore Toledo for weeks, and continually find new treasures in the remains of buildings and ruins that abound, and there is more work for artists of the Prout school than in any city that we have ever visited.

'Pictures are here ready made, no composition is needed. What could be better, for instance, than a string of mules betasselled and bedizened with gay-coloured trappings, laden with the quaint old water-jars, lazily plodding their way along the sunny road leading from under the grand old Moorish gate (the "Puerta del Sol" of Toledo), picturesque ruins on one side, and the Tagus, winding far away beneath, on the other—the colour of everything almost oriental?'

Taking a mule, the only means of conveyance for those who cannot walk, a more interesting day cannot be spent than (having seen the sights and done one's duty as a tourist) quietly and without a guide to explore the byways and 'nooks and corners,' stopping anywhere by chance to purchase the curious trinkets and ornaments to be found in the *old* shops. No one seems to care to sell you anything, and you feel yourself rather in the position of one asking, than conferring, a favour, when, getting off your mule, you stumble into one of these little dark recesses and offer to make a purchase. The proprietor, whom you have possibly disturbed in a 'siesta,' immediately lights a *cigarito* and rouses himself to watch your proceedings; but he offers you nothing, and seems relieved when you have taken your departure.

At the end of the day you have lost yourself of course, but there is no need for any anxiety: let the mule find his own way, and the chances are you will arrive at the door of your *Fonda* in two or three minutes, and that you have been close to it for the last two or three hours!

We reserved our visits to the cathedral until the last. It stands, it is said, on the site of the ancient *Santa Maria*, which was built about the year 600, and afterwards converted into a mosque when the Moors held possession of Toledo. It was again changed into a cathedral in 1086, and in the year 1227 was totally destroyed by Don Fernando III.

The present edifice was commenced A.D. 1227, and was not completed until the commencement of the eighteenth century, if it may be said to be

completed even now. Its style, according to
good authorities, 'belongs to the best period of
pointed Gothic, with here and there a few exceptions appertaining to the Gothic of the fifteenth
or florid decline.' As at Burgos, we were unable
to obtain any good exterior view, owing to the
crowd of buildings with which it is surrounded,
and it was only from one side of the *Plaza del
Ayuntamiento* that we could see even the façade
to advantage, with its beautiful stone carving.
The cathedral is generally approached by the
'*Calle de la Chapineria*,' from which the spire is
well seen.

The plan of the building is on an enormous
scale, larger than almost any cathedral in Christendom; its length is 400 feet, and width 200
feet. The interior is divided into five naves,
besides the chapels on the eastern side, the centre
being more than 100 feet in height. There are
750 stained glass windows, two of them large
'rose' windows of great beauty and richness.
The *coro* or choir, the screen of which prevents
one obtaining any good general view, is in itself
a magnificent work, rivalling Chartres in its design, but not in delicacy of workmanship. Mr.
Street, whose book should be referred to for a
complete account of the interior of this cathe-

dral,[1] draws particular attention to the beauty of the carving in the choir, and has given a detailed account of the subjects on the screens, adding, 'I feel the more bound to do this, because in the Spanish guide-books they are spoken of with the utmost contempt, whilst all the praise is reserved for a vile gilt creation by Berruguete, which has taken the place of three central western subjects over the choir door, and for two statues of Innocence and Sin, which seem to me to be innocent of art, and to sin against nature!'

The floor of the *coro* is of red and white marble, and the stalls (of which there are fifty, in two rows) are elaborately carved both above and beneath, in walnut-wood, in every variety of subject and design. In the centre is an enormous brass eagle (lectern), with wings outstretched, fighting a dragon.

The Gothic 'retablo,' which reaches to the roof in the 'capilla mayor,' is one of the most noticeable works. It is approached by steps of jasper, and is crowded with groups of carving representing scenes from the life of our Saviour, &c. The figures are richly painted and gilt, and the general effect is magnificent, being an excellent

---

[1] Gothic Architecture in Spain, p. 495.

example of the successful use of colour and gold in Gothic work.

We examined the numerous chapels, the tombs, and the beautiful carving, and afterwards endeavoured to see the 'treasures' of the cathedral, which are said to be very great, and to exceed in value the public treasury! Permission was politely refused, as 'a robbery had lately taken place' in the sacristy. We were shown a number of relics, and skulls and bones tied with ribbons and adorned with precious jewels; also the stone that 'the Virgin Mary stepped upon when she appeared to San Ildefonso.' It is enclosed in an iron grating, and is worn down, not with feet, but with the hands of thousands of the faithful and the curious.

We had heard and read much of this cathedral, as being one of the glories of Spain, but were quite unprepared for a scene of such grandeur and magnificence. It is impossible to give any adequate idea of it in our short notes; but before leaving, we must speak of one curious 'effect' in the interior.

Entering the building by the north door, towards evening, when it is half in gloom, we have not approached the 'coro' many paces, when suddenly behind it we see a flood of warm light, darting in bright rays, as it were, through the roof, and through which forms of saints and angels are seen descending. The figures appear the size of life, and in the strange light have a startling effect of reality. Architecturally, it is doubtless a 'mistake,' but it is impressive and striking at first sight, and is, we believe, unlike anything in any other Gothic cathedral in the world.

To the uneducated mind—to those to whom religion is taught by impressions—to the women we see kneeling beneath the dome, it is a picture (speaking to them in a language they can understand) of the glories of another world. They are happily ignorant that what they regard with wonder and reverence is almost universally condemned as a 'theatrical monstrosity' and an 'architectural solecism.'

We returned to Madrid by the same route, carrying away with us a few relics, and *not* any Toledo blades. The latter are manufactured in large quantities to sell to visitors, and are generally worthless. As some one suggests of the worthy (or unworthy) vendors of these goods—'Their blood's Castilian, but their blade's *cast* steel'— and certainly the stilettos and daggers offered for

sale at high prices, were not worth the trouble of carrying away. At the old manufactory, situated about a mile from the town, a genuine Toledan sword can be purchased, but they are seldom to be met with anywhere else.

CHAPTER VIII.

MADRID TO CORDOVA.

'Swallow, swallow, flying, flying south,
Fly to her, and fall upon her gilded eaves,
And tell her—what I tell to thee.'—*Tennyson's Princess.*

O swallows flying from England's wintry winds, who, when summer is over, disperse like autumn leaves—to those who, dreading the sea passage to the south of Spain, think the overland route would be preferable, this chapter is dedicated. The general reader may pass it over as a mere chapter of accidents, that would never have been printed, had not we been assured by many friends that what happened to our party is occurring every day, and ought to be made known.

We were disposed to attribute the little mishaps on this journey chiefly to our own inexperience or blundering, but we have since learned that such events are part of a system, and that everything connected with the route is going from bad to worse.

Taking up a London newspaper in the month of March, 1866, we find this railway, and its Madrid terminus, described, as it were only yesterday, precisely in the state that we found it a year and a half ago; and which we then attributed to the fact that the line had only just been opened for traffic.

'The arrangements of a Spanish railway station are peculiar, and thoroughly unlike anything else in the world. There is no newspaper or bookstall, no refreshment-room, and no one to give you any information. The waiting-rooms are not opened until shortly before the starting of the train; there are no benches in the outer hall.

'At the Madrid terminus, first, second, and third class tickets are dispensed from the same hutch. The last-named class of carriages are the equipages of soldiers and peasants, who carry their luggage in their hands. But as the burden frequently includes a jar or a gourd of water, a bundle of blankets, a baby, a pot and a pan or so, a basket of provisions, and, in some cases, a mattress, to say nothing of muskets, swords, knapsacks, and canteens, it is no easy matter to get close enough to the hutch to obtain a ticket.

'The solitary waiting-room was a most miserable hole, the door off its hinges, the range rusting in the fireplace, the garish French paper stripped from the walls, the windows looking on the platform all broken, the tiled floor half untiled and showing the bare earth. There was not a chair or a table, and the flaring gas-burner had neither chimney nor globe. That every one should be smoking, also, is a fact which constantly recorded can only prove wearisome. It is "*un costumbre del pais.*"

'When at last I struggled on to the platform, where there were neither guards nor porters, I got into the first carriage I could find haphazard, in the hope that it belonged to that portion of the train bound towards Cordova. As it was, I happened to have entered a carriage going not to Cordova, but to Valencia and Alicante; *fortunately*, just before we reached Alcazar, where the line branches off, a goodnatured Spanish officer, with whom I had been talking in the early part of the evening, woke me up from a sound slumber and told me I must change my place.'

On the 17th of October, 1864, our party, consisting of two English and one French lady, and two gentlemen, left Madrid for Cordova. Having been occupied from 6 P.M. until past 9 in making arrangements for departure, fighting against extortion and exorbitant demands for money for carriages, luggage, porters, &c.; and having been kept standing more than an hour at the terminus, we were glad enough to reach our railway carriage and rest. Thankful were we to hear ourselves locked up, and to be left in peace, even with a prospect of a journey of two nights and a day without stopping. The carriage was, of course, quite full, and the windows were all closed. Our fellow travellers smoked hard, but before long we all fell asleep. No one disturbed us during the night, and nearly all the stations were in darkness.

When the grey morning light appeared, we began to arouse ourselves and look about us, and mutual congratulations were exchanged on having got so well through the night, when some one observed that 'the country was rather flat for the Sierra Morena,' and that 'by the time (5 A.M.) we ought to be near Santa Cruz.' Suddenly the awkward fact dawned upon us, we had come by the wrong line, and had nearly arrived at Alicante!

Oh! for a 'goodnatured Spanish officer' to have told us, what was not then stated in any guide-book, nor on our tickets, nor on the railway time-table, and what our goodnatured Spanish friends who came to see us off at Madrid had also omitted to mention, that we should '*change carriages at Alcazar.*'

Oct. 18. 'Here we are at half-past 5 in the morning, at Chinchilla, near Alicante. There is only a small station, no house in sight, and no means of getting away until about 12 at noon, when the return train passes, going to Madrid. Luckily we have a piece of bread and a little chocolate, which we divide amongst us. It is raining heavily, and there is nothing to be done but to wait quietly in the little damp shed, with its muddy floor.'

The wall was adorned with the following time-table, which, as a specimen of the 'official' railway guide, and an indication of the important traffic between the two chief cities of a European state, is, we should think, unique. There is, it will be observed, not much to guide the traveller as to where, or when, to change from one line to another.

Servicio desde el 1.º de Mayo de 1864	LINEA DE MADRID A CORDOBA.[1]							
DE MADRID A SANTA CRUZ.					DE SANTA CRUZ A MADRID.			
ESTACIONES.	TREN MIXTO. Todas clases.		TREN MIXTO. Todas clases.		ESTACIONES.	TREN MIXTO. Todas clases.		TREN MIXTO. Todas clases.
	Llegada.	Salida.	Llegada.	Salida.		Llegada.	Salida.	Llegada.	Salida.
MADRID ...	"	M. 7 "	"	N. 8 55	SANTA CRUZ	M. "	"	"	N. 9 35
Alcazar	"	12 30	1 01	1 59	Valdepenas...	12 56	12 25	10 "	10 12
Argamasilla ..	1 23	1 28	2 43	2 48	Manzanares ..	2 03	1 08	11 "	11 15
Manzanares ..	2 17	2 27	3 29	3 39	Argamasilla ..	3 07	2 18	11 56	12 01
Valdepenas...	3 24	3 34	4 28	4 38	Alcazar......	4 05	3 12	12 45	1 59
SANTA CRUZ	4 54	"	5 04	"	MADRID ...	9 40	4 41 N.	6 40 M.	"
	T.								

There was no telegraph, and no means of communicating with Madrid or Santa Cruz; so that we could only wait quietly for seven hours, and then (by paying again) return to Alcazar, a distance of about 100 miles.

About five in the afternoon we again arrived at Alcazar, and dined: we mention this because it was the only decent meal we had for four days. Here we had to wait until two o'clock on the follow-

---

[1] This line is now near completion; but there are still sixty miles of diligence travelling between the two cities. April, 1866.

ing morning, when the train for Santa Cruz would arrive. Our luggage, books, sketching-blocks, &c., had, of course, all gone on to Cordova.

We explored the town and neighbourhood, as well as we could in the dark, to see if there were any "Ventas," but they were less tolerable, and there was less chance of obtaining any rest or quiet, of which some of our party began to stand in need, than in the railway station itself, which was worse in its want of accommodation and in its company than the one at Madrid.

At 5 A.M. we reached 'Santa Cruz,' where the railway ended. It turned out just as we expected, we had forfeited our seats in the '*diligencia*,' and there were now none to be had, even by paying over again.

The shed which has done duty as a terminus here for many years was even worse than Alcazar. The interior was one common room, in which were crowded passengers, porters, and postboys; but it was chiefly filled with beggars (who seem to have free admission everywhere), representing in their persons half the calendar of human ills, and thrusting themselves and their filthy garments into every one's notice.

The air was suffocating, and the noise and confusion tremendous. Outside, the rain was pouring down, and the road, or open space where the diligences stood ready to start, was nearly a foot deep in liquid mud.

When those who were fortunate enough to have secured places had departed, we telegraphed to our friends in Madrid to engage others for us for the next morning, and then waded through the mud and water to a low building (like an Irish mud cabin, and by courtesy called a '*Venta*'), to see if we could get accommodation for the night. We did—in a room measuring about five feet square, with a small hole in the wall to admit light. It was situated just over the 'comedar,' or eating-room, which we could see between the planks of the floor. Here we spent the day and night, chiefly occupied in endeavouring to keep out the rain that poured through the roof.

The night was a terrible one, the wind swept down in fierce gusts from the Sierra Morena, and the rain scarcely ever ceased. We sat round the brazeros, in order to keep, if not dry, at least tolerably warm, and made ourselves 'jolly' under circumstances that would have done credit to Mark Tapley. The people were civil, and did the best they could for us (and for themselves) during our stay—the former in giving us excellent chocolate and bread, the latter in presenting us with a bill as if we had dined at the '*Trois Frères*' in Paris.

It was edifying under these circumstances, and to while away the time, to read Hans Andersen's description of Santa Cruz, written a year or two previously:—

'I have not seen so dirty a town in the whole of Spain. The streets were unpaved, and covered with thick bad-smelling mud. It was impossible to walk, still less to live here; the houses were all poor miserable huts.

'Some little distance from the town was situated a *Fonda*, which had been recommended to us, and was, indeed, the only one in the place. It looked by no means inviting; it was a large dirty tavern, with low dingy rooms, upon the floors of which straw had been strewed to keep the feet warm. Our bedroom, the best in the house, had no window, only an opening in the wall with a wooden grating.

'To have passed the night here, and to have spent the whole of the following afternoon in this hole, would have been impossible. No, I would rather faint or die in the railway carriage from over fatigue!'

Our hovel was packed pretty closely that night, judging from the number of separate and distinct snores that we heard within a few inches of us, both above and below, and on each side; but we will not go into any further details, some of which could not be written down.

Santa Cruz is the only halting-place between Madrid and Cordova, but travellers are forewarned not to stop here. It may be said, therefore, that 'whatever we experienced we brought upon ourselves,' and that it was 'our own fault.' We can only reply that those who have not been in Spain can form no idea how easy it is, even with a knowledge of the language, to make a mistake on their railways in the middle of the night, with scarcely any lights or names displayed at the stations; and that, if it was a 'fault,' it is fast becoming a '*custom*,' judging from the numbers of travellers who have done the same thing.

We did not know until afterwards, that the practice of omitting to put 'change at Alcazar' on their tickets, was a source of considerable revenue to the 'diligence companies,' and that no sooner have travellers passed the junction, than a message is sent to Santa Cruz, which being translated might read, 'It's all right; five passengers gone towards Alicante; fill up their seats in the berlina!'

At 5 on Thursday morning (we left Madrid on Monday night) we again presented ourselves at the 'office,' hoping that our friends—who had not replied to our telegram, although we had paid for an answer—had secured places for us. We were assured that none had been taken, but that, if we liked to separate, seats might possibly be found. The case was a desperate one: we could not stay another night at Santa Cruz, and so we paid for five more places.

There were several diligences (great lumbering conveyances covered with mud, of which it would be difficult to say whether they were dirtier inside or out) drawn up in line near the railway, in the middle of a pond, with their gaily caparisoned team of mules standing up to their knees in water. Seats were at last found for the ladies of our party in the '*intérieur*' and in the '*banquette*' on the top; the rest rode where they could, one with the driver on one diligence, and the other with the luggage on the roof of another.

A Spanish '*diligencia*' holds between twenty and thirty people, besides luggage and merchandise. On the chief high roads it is drawn by a team of ten or twelve mules, the country being hilly, and the roads heavy. They are harnessed two abreast, a boy riding on one of the leaders, and it is on his care, and the sagacity of the animals, that the guidance and safety of the vehicle depend. The driver holds loosely the reins of the two last, but he has little or no power to guide or control the movements of the vehicle with such a team, and it is only fair to say that he seldom attempts it.

Each diligence is accompanied by a '*mayoral*,'

or conductor, a very important personage, who has charge of the whole equipage, and who, with his embroidered jacket and gaiters with silver buttons, his red sash, and bright handkerchief round his head, is here, there, and everywhere during the journey; and if, as is generally the case, he is a jolly fellow, he is the life of the party. He has the important office of assigning the passengers their seats, and deciding the time and the place where the diligence is to stop.

There is a coupé, called a '*berlina*,' holding three people; an '*intéricur*,' a '*rotonde*,' and a '*banquette*' above, called a '*coupé*,' with seats for three or four. The roof is a sort of warehouse, where passengers' luggage and merchandise are stowed away, including provisions of all kinds, both alive and dead. When all other seats are taken, passengers are packed away on the roof, and often have an exciting time of it in warding off the charges of portmanteaus and boxes as the diligence sways from side to side, and when it becomes dark, as may be imagined, the combat thickens.

The pace is generally good, averaging eight miles an hour, including hills and short stoppages. But the roads are falling into neglect and disuse, and in many places between Madrid and Cordova the railway has destroyed the old road without leaving any substitute. The theory is, that, as there will soon be railway communication, it is useless to keep up the roads; and as it will still be years (if ever) before the line is completed, between the two the diligence sticks in the mud.

Accidents happen continually, but they are seldom serious, and are taken as a matter of course. As far as our experience goes, the chances are about equal as to whether you arrive at your journey's end without some sort of *contretemps*. A common one is this: The diligence is approaching a town after a long day, coming down hill at a swinging trot, at the rate of about ten miles an hour, sometimes even faster, for the Spaniard is like the traditional English postboy, who always reserved a gallop for the last mile; the postilion, who has perhaps been in the saddle for twenty or thirty hours without rest, takes this opportunity to doze, or more frequently to drop the reins, and concentrate his whole attention upon making a new thong to his whip. Suddenly his horse stumbles and falls; away rolls the postboy into a ditch or down an embankment; down go the mules, tumbling over and over one another, and pile up in an instant into a dusty, struggling heap, upon the top of which the heavy diligence rolls, and there stops, or falls, as sometimes happens, over on one side.

The scene of uproar and confusion that ensues can hardly be described. The struggles of the mules to extricate themselves, and of the passengers to get clear of their heels; the shouting and yelling of the driver and postboys; the groans of the wounded animals, who are often crushed under the diligence; and the apparently inextricable confusion of everything, must indeed be witnessed to be understood. Sometimes the diligence has to be unloaded, and some of the mules taken out of the team, causing a delay of several hours; but the journey is generally accomplished without any more serious mishap than a stunned postboy, or two or three mules left dead on the roadside.

It is very amusing, before it becomes monotonous, to sit in the *coupé*, or *berlina*, and listen to the compliments, threats, and expostulations in turn of the driver (called the '*moto*'), who has charge of the team, and who is perpetually jumping down and running by the side to keep them in a trot. Every animal has a name, and answers to it; and if the 'mayoral' happens to mention to the driver in a low tone that 'Brunella,' or 'Zitella,' or some other delinquent, is not pulling properly,

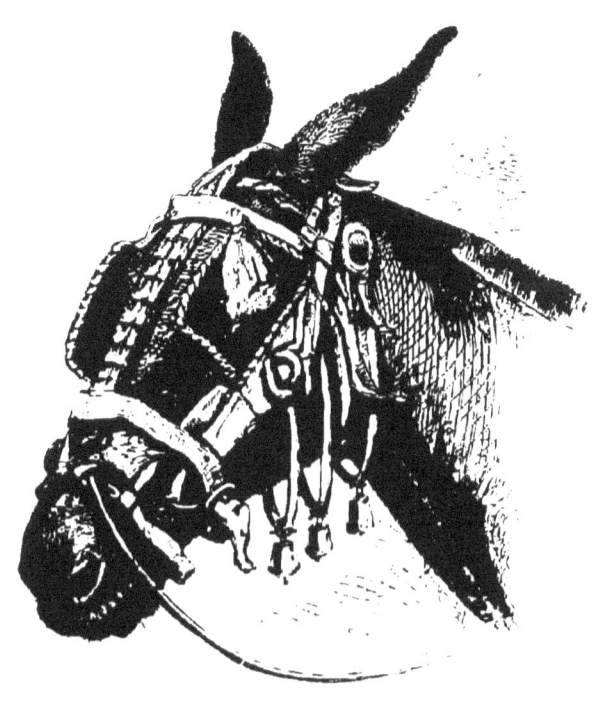

she immediately begins tugging and struggling as if she were doing half the work of the team: 'Brunella' probably remembering well the penalty for nonfulfilment of duty, her tender driver thinking nothing of getting down and picking a handful of the sharpest stones that he can find and throwing them at the animal's head.

At the stages where they change they often get into the greatest confusion, and much time is lost. Just as you are dozing, or in the middle of the night, you become gradually conscious of a sound of scuffling, shouting, and swearing, and the free use, apparently, of the names of all the saints in the calendar, and you wake up to find the nose of a mule rubbing against your window, and that he has his fore feet on the body of another lying on the ground; and gradually, by the light of a lantern, you discover the whole team tied into an apparently inextricable knot, whilst the excited drivers are struggling to get them into line again.

But to proceed with our journey. We started in a long procession through the narrow streets of Santa Cruz, the mules sinking to their girths in the soft mud. Directly we got out of the town we kept up a quick trot, which, soon increasing to a gallop, made the overladen diligence swing from side to side, and creak and groan in every part.

The ride over the Sierra Morena was very beautiful; the scenery wild and rugged; with few trees and little cultivation until we descended the southern slopes. At every few miles we passed railway works, which seemed to be making little progress; there were iron bridges, arches, and buttresses, which foreign contractors had put up years ago, standing waiting for the earthworks and embankments to be filled up, and looking as if they would fall before the Spaniards were likely to finish them.

The morning was fine, with a very cold wind, and the road being harder as we ascended and descended the slopes of the Sierra Morena, we rattled along gaily. We had gone about thirty miles, and were congratulating ourselves upon at last being well on our way, when suddenly some one suggested that one of the wheels of our diligence 'looked as if it were coming off.'

On one side of us was a wall of rock, on the other a deep ravine, and we were at the time going rapidly down hill. We shouted to the 'mayoral,' who at first pretended not to hear us, but in a short time he called to the driver and postboy, who brought the diligence to a stand.

We were first in the procession, and when we drew up to the side of the road, the other diligences rushed past us at a gallop and were soon out of sight. The wheel was not coming off, but the *tire was off*, and the wheel was rapidly going to pieces.

There was a long consultation, but nothing was done, and finally the passengers were quietly informed that if they would wait a little 'the postilion should fetch another wheel.' There was of course nothing to do but to submit, and we soon saw the postilion gallop back towards Santa Cruz; and the 'mayoral,' the driver, and his team of mules, disappear in another direction.

The spot where the accident happened was desolate, and exposed to the wind, but the morning being fine, and the passengers in good humour, we all strolled about on the mountain to pass away the time. There was no dwelling within sight, but after walking some distance we came to a rude wayside hut, with mules stalled at one end, and two or three people warming themselves at a 'brazero' at the other.

It was about ten A.M. when the accident occurred; and as we were expecting to have to start again at any minute, we did not like to wander very far. In the middle of the day we all clubbed together, and shared what provisions we happened to have brought with us. The travellers, who were English, American, French, and Spaniards, were all very sociable round the fire, and enjoyed the novelty of the scene.

But as evening approached, and the sun went down without any sign of our 'mayoral,' it looked more serious, and we began to consider whether it would not be better to walk to the nearest town, to seek shelter for the night. However, in Spain, as in the East, there is very little twilight, and we soon found ourselves in total darkness; there was then no resource but for each passenger to find his way, as best he could, back to his own seat in the diligence, and try to go to sleep.

By seven o'clock we all 'turned in,' and strange indeed it seemed to be perched up in a diligence in the darkness, on a bleak mountain side; the only sound the whistling of the wind and the pattering of dust and small stones against the window-panes. Every one smoked until he went to sleep, and the diligence sent up a 'volume' all through the night. Occasionally the moon shone out between passing clouds, and we could distinguish our route winding round the mountain far below us, in places so very steep and apparently precipitous, that we all agreed that it would be better to wait for daylight, even if assistance came before the morning. We therefore resigned ourselves to our fate, wrapped ourselves up as best we could, and waited for the morning.

But in Spain it is difficult to foresee what will happen. At about two o'clock in the morning, when most of us had gone to sleep, we were suddenly aroused by what appeared to our sleepy senses to be first an earthquake, and then as if the diligence were trying to turn over and rid itself of its burden. Clouds had again obscured the moon, and it was quite dark, and for some time we could make out nothing: but on getting down we found our driver and postilion had just returned with a wheel, and, with the aid of some men they had brought with them, were endeavouring to hoist up the diligence with its heavy burden, in order to fix on the new wheel which the boy had just brought, riding all the way from Santa Cruz with it hanging round his neck, with his head sticking between the spokes!

It was, of course, impossible to do anything without unloading the diligence, and so, by the dim light of one candle in a lantern, all the shivering figures had to turn out, and crouch together by the road-side, whilst the operation was being performed. The *wheel fitted*, and great was the shout of rejoicing thereupon.

In about an hour we were getting up into our seats again, when a tremendous noise of scuffling of feet and shouting was heard in the darkness near us. It turned out that the team of mules had started off down the mountain, dragging with them the boy who had been placed in charge. Then of course there was a grand chase, and they were finally brought back in a desperate state of entanglement and confusion. This caused another delay of nearly an hour, by which time many of us had again gone to sleep, when the signal was given to start. With a lurch and a crash (occasioned by our being pulled off the 'jack,' or lever, on which the diligence rested whilst the wheel was being fitted, tearing it to pieces by dragging the vehicle over it, because no one had taken the trouble to move it away), we started at once into a gallop, several of the animals having their legs over the traces, and for three or four hours without a halt kept rushing through the darkness: sometimes jolting against a bank, and 'shipping' earth and stones, and swinging from side to side in a manner which would have sent us all out of our seats if we had not been closely packed.

The rain now fell heavily, and we were soon ploughing through mud and crossing torrents, which made the latter part of our progress very slow and tedious. As we got farther south and began to descend, the air became much softer, the vegetation altered with the change of climate, and aloes and the prickly cactus grew on the road-side. We passed one or two towns of no great interest, and made our only halt at Bailen— a poor, dull, neglected-looking town, containing, it is said, but we can scarcely credit it, about 10,000 inhabitants—and finally reached Cordova on Friday evening; being four days and nights since we had left Madrid, without taking off our clothes or entering a decent habitation. The other travellers arrived at Cordova on Friday morning, not knowing what had detained us, and supposing all the while that we were close behind.

We were not yet 'out of the wood;' a few days afterwards we received a letter from our friends in Madrid, requesting us to forward immediately the sum of 13*l.*, which had been paid for a *third* set of places taken for us several days after we had telegraphed for them! The dear, good, kind people thought probably, as all Spaniards do, that there was no hurry, and put off securing the places until—*mañana!*

CHAPTER IX.

CORDOVA.

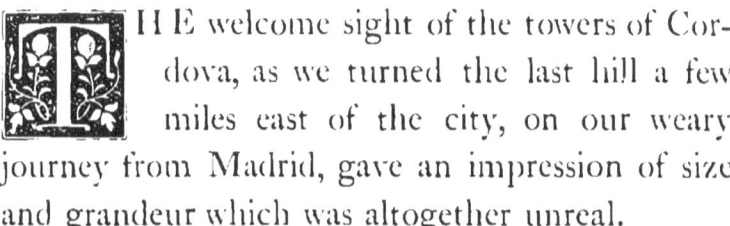THE welcome sight of the towers of Cordova, as we turned the last hill a few miles east of the city, on our weary journey from Madrid, gave an impression of size and grandeur which was altogether unreal.

As we approached its gates, the great mosque with its Moorish battlements and ' Catholic dome,' towering above all other buildings, showed us at one glance where the chief objects of interest in Cordova were centered: but the most imposing entrance into this city is from the south, by the road from Malaga and Ecija, crossing the Guadalquivir, near the ruins of an aqueduct and close to the walls of the mosque, which, from this point of view, appears like a town in itself.

When we look out of our window at the '*Fonda Rizzi*' the next morning, we find a half-ruined half-deserted city. The houses are white and flat-roofed, the air is soft and balmy; we can see orange-gardens and 'patios' filled with exotic plants, and the aspect is altogether Oriental. There are several palm-trees in the city, and in the distance olive-groves and fertile plains, through which we can trace the windings of the river Guadalquivir. The '*Fonda Rizzi*' is situated near the centre of the city on high ground, and from our windows, which are at the back, there is a very extensive view. Our sketch, taken from this window, comprises only a small portion of the scene, and wants colour to give it the proper effect; but it is faithful as far as it goes.

The aspect of the city when we walk through it is in keeping with its outward appearance. There is very little sign of bustle and activity, and here, as at Toledo, the only life it exhibits seems to be owing to the constant passage of travellers between Madrid and Seville. The manufacture of the famous Cordova leather is almost a thing of the past, although they are still at work in a few factories. The public buildings and the churches give evidence of poverty and neglect, and are not architecturally interesting; and it is only when we come to the mosque and the remains of Moorish buildings that we feel rewarded for the journey.

SAN JOSÉ FROM THE 'PONTA LARGA,' CORVO.

Directly on leaving the '*Fonda*' we find ourselves shut in, in a series of narrow courts or alleys, so narrow that we can touch both sides at once. The walls of the houses are whitewashed, with little barred windows looking on to the street. In purely Oriental towns the charm of these little windows is, that they are often the framework of a magnificent pair of eyes that dart their glances upon the passers by; many of these windows were once so illuminated, but times have sadly changed.

We have no time for a reverie—a string of donkeys laden with paniers containing merchandise and fruits of all kinds; live fowls hanging down, a dozen together tied by the leg on one side and two or three little lambs on the other, thrown across a donkey's back like a sack, the cavalcade driven by muleteers in gay sashes, embroidered gaiters, and velvet hats; followed by water-carriers, men and women,—make us beat a retreat into the nearest doorway to let them pass. Following them to the 'Plaza,' or market-place, a large neglected-looking square, with arcades chiefly appropriated to tinkers' and Jews' clothes-shops, we see what little there is left of native costume in Cordova. Its appearance, to tell the truth, is most dilapidated and 'seedy'—there is no better word. Italians are much more picturesque than the groups we see here, and are more consistent in their dress.

The *Señoras* wear a red rose or sprig of jessamine in their hair, and throw a mantilla over their heads (because, we presume, they know, intuitively, that it is more becoming to them than a bonnet); but their dresses come from Lyons or Marseilles; and the poorer classes imitate their betters and buy all the modern finery they can.

A few of the old nobility still reside in Cordova and its environs, and it is fair to presume that that old lady that we see nearly every day, bumped and jolted over the stones through the few wide and illpaved streets of which Cordova can boast, is a representative of some ancient house: she has imported a new open carriage from Madrid, and it is evident that the cobblestones and the rather unscientific 'whip,' who is belabouring the mules that complete the equipage, will make short work with the springs. She is going to take her daily ride on the 'alameda,' and *promenade* alone by the banks of the Guadalquivir.

Everything about the city had a dreamy forsaken look, and a forsaken sound. Even at Toledo we sometimes heard the tones of the guitar, but at Cordova scarcely ever. From the few people that we saw altogether during our visit, it hardly seemed possible that the city should contain at the present time 40,000 inhabitants; and quite in the region of romance and fable that this same Cordova was once the 'largest city in the western world, that it measured twenty-four miles by six, the whole space covered with houses, palaces, mosques, and gardens, down to the banks of the Guadalquivir.'

We read that, 'outside Cordova, there were 3000 towns and villages appertaining to it,' that 'there was no city comparable to it, either with respect to population, extent of buildings, size of markets, cleanliness of streets, religious edifices, or number of its baths and inns, and that in point of magnitude it approached the famous city of Bagdad;' that 'the people were renowned for the elegance of their dress, attention to religious duties, pride in their great mosque, and glory in nobility of descent, as well as in warlike enterprise and science;' also that Cordova 'possessed a greater abundance of books than any other city of Spain, and its inhabitants were amongst the most impassioned collectors in the world.'

What a contrast to learn from our 'Murray' that 'Cordova is now a poor Bœotian place, the residence of local authorities, with a 'liceo,' theatre, 'casa de espositos,' 'plaza de toros,' and a national 'museo' with some rubbish in San Pablo, and a library of no particular consequence—a day will amply suffice to see everything!"

There was really little to see besides the mosque, which we went to every day. It occupies an immense area, surrounded by a high wall of Moorish work. We enter first (under a horseshoe arch) the 'Court of Oranges,' an oblong court or garden, upwards of 400 feet long, with trees and fountains in the centre. Nothing can exceed the beauty of this court, with its orange-trees, palms, and cypresses. To come suddenly out of the glare of the burning streets into the cool shade, where fountains are playing, birds singing, and breezes bearing upon them the most delicious odours, is what we read of in the 'Arabian Nights,' but seldom realise. Our sketch gives but an imperfect idea of its appearance, because we are unable to show much of the walls of the mosque which surround it and completely shut off all sight or sound of the city.

The first sight of the interior of this extraordinary place of worship is utterly unlike that of any other building in Western Europe. It has a very low roof, with the familiar horseshoe arch, sup-

COURT, BISHOP'S, CORDOVA

ported by a perfect forest of marble pillars. The area of the interior is 642 feet by 462, and the roof cannot in some places be more than 30 feet high. Near the centre there is a lofty *capilla*, erected by the Christians when the mosque was first used as a cathedral. In this—especially in the 'coro'—there is some fine carving; and also in a number of side chapels, dedicated to various saints.

There are some 'treasures' in the sacristy, but not of great value, and scarcely worth the trouble of searching out. The real treasures are in the variety and beauty of the Moorish ornamentation to be met with at every turn, some of which is in excellent preservation.

When the Moslem population divided the building with the Christians, they religiously abstained from imitating any of their work, and thus, as at Toledo, we observe the distinctive character of the two styles of architecture, side by side.

What this edifice must have been when, as historians tell us, 'its roof was higher and glistened with gilding and vivid colours, and thousands of gold and silver lamps—when its walls were worked like lace and looked like cashmere shawls illuminated from behind, and its arches, like so many gigantic bows, studded with emeralds and rubies, resting on mosaic trunks of porphyry, jasper, and other precious marbles,' could not be imagined from any description of its appearance now, when it is only here and there that we can trace out a complete design, and from under a coating of whitewash discover distinct traces of its former glory. There is little colour excepting in the chapels, and most of the glitter and brightness that we see now is modern and 'catholic' work.

The simplicity and massive grandeur of the mosque are its most striking features, and leave an impression on the mind long after the recollection of details has passed away.

Before leaving Cordova we must say a word about the '*Fonda Rizzi.*' It had a delightful courtyard in the centre, planted with flowers, surrounded by arcades supported by marble pillars; and there was a gallery above, upon which the rooms opened, and the view from one or two of the back windows was superb. Our rooms were tolerably well furnished, and were light and airy; but the charges were high, the living was bad, and the attendance —*nil.* Our bedrooms, for instance, seemed as if they had never been cleaned since the Moors held possession of Cordova, and a night's rest was impossible.

On the morning of our departure it was no difficult matter to rise at five; but it was almost impossible to persuade any one (especially a Spaniard) that it was necessary to depart by the early morning train. The whole household was in a conspiracy to make us spend another day at Cordova; but by dint of being inflexible, and persistently misunderstanding information about the trains that we knew to be erroneous, we carried our point, and in a thick wet fog, as dense and penetrating as anything that we experience in England, we were conducted in the darkness through the silent streets, by a porter with a small lantern, to the *despacho* or office, where we were consigned to a damp omnibus, which deposited us at the railway station just one hour and a quarter before the required time.

It soon began to rain, and when it was daylight the fog and mist hung low in the valleys, and intercepted any distant view. However, there is very little to see on this journey, and no towns of importance are passed.

Just before we arrived at Seville it rained, literally in torrents. The railway station is a miserable shed, with the roof adjusted on the Madrid street-pattern, with the water pouring off upon the pathway. There were a number of passengers, who rushed for shelter into an enormous omnibus, and filled it so that we had a line of people standing down the middle. The vehicle was judiciously placed under the edge of the roof, and received a perfect waterspout, which penetrating through the top of the omnibus soon began to fill it. We had to sit in this plight for about half an hour, whilst baggage was being examined. All this would not be worth recounting were it not so characteristic of the country, and a good example of what is continually happening, without any attempt at amendment.

Travellers who are putting off a visit to Spain for two or three years, hoping that then these things will be improved, may rest assured that whenever they come 'improvements' will be put off a little longer. The same stones that nearly overturned our diligence on the Sierra Morena, were lying across the road as we passed on our return journey, and they are there still, unless a foreigner has moved them.

CHAPTER X.

SEVILLE.

OUR first impressions of Seville were those of disappointment. As we drove through it we had glimpses of the noble tower '*La Giralda*,' of which we have endeavoured to give the reader some idea in the next illustration; and we knew that in its cathedral, its '*Alcazar*,' its collection of pictures, and in its associations, there were few cities to compare with it for interest—still, it fell far short of our anticipations.

The houses are low, the streets are very narrow and badly paved, and there is no rising ground from which to get any good general view.

'From the balcony of the '*Fonda de Paris*,' in the 'Plaza de Magdalena,' we can see something of the city and its inhabitants. There is a little stall underneath our window where more cold water has been sold and consumed than we ever saw distributed gratis within the same space of time at any public pump. The little bell tinkles incessantly, and the cry of "*agua*," "*agua*," is kept up all day—water, with a dash of sugar in it for the more luxurious—seems to be the 'staff of life.'

'And what are the inhabitants like? Curiously like the rest of the civilized world, and with little variation in dress from our own people. The man who sells the water is a little gayer in his attire, and his hair is trimmed with a delicate pigtail like the Madrid dandies. His customers are, from Murillo's dirty street-boys, upwards to grave *señores* in cloaks and bright-red umbrellas, embroidered with black. *Las señoras* wear the mantilla almost always, and very few bonnets are to be seen.

'The buildings are substantial and bright looking, with plain whitewashed walls, and court-yards opening to the street. There is much bustle and apparent business in the principal streets, and the shops are filled with French and foreign goods.'

Our first visit was to the Cathedral, in the morning when the sun was high, as we had been forewarned that this was the only time when the pictures could be well seen.

The Cathedral, the Court of Oranges, with

the chapter and offices, form a square pile of great extent, raised upon a platform or terrace. In the illustration we have given the best view of the '*Giralda*,' and part of the Gothic Cathedral, which, as we approach it through narrow crowded streets, is seen towering above all other buildings. Those who have heard in Mahommedan countries the muezzin's cry from the towers of a mosque, calling upon the faithful to 'come to prayers, come to prayers, it is better to pray than to sleep,' cannot help thinking of that time, when 'Seville was the beloved city of the Moslem—the gold and lace tent of the sensual eastern—who planted it on the banks of the Guadalquivir to dream life away amid the enchantments of refined taste, which he lavished his gold and genius to adorn, and his blood to defend and fortify.'

Nothing that we have yet seen in Spain brings more vividly before us the colossal scale on which the Moors worked than '*La Giralda*,' which is a square Moorish tower, about 350 feet in height, ascended by a series of inclined planes, like the tower of St. Mark's at Venice: it is about the same height, and was built at the same period. Remains of Moorish ornamentation may be traced upon it, but the upper part, the belfry, and the bronze figure of 'Faith' on the top, are modern additions.

From this tower we obtain our only good view of Seville. We can distinguish a few of the principal streets and plazas; and the terraced houses, with their pretty balconies and green patios, but the buildings are so close to each other that they almost seem to touch. Immediately beneath is the Gothic cathedral, with its pinnacles and enormous roof with flying buttresses; near it is the *Alcazar*, the old Moorish palace, with its beautiful courts and gardens, extending as they once did to the river-side, to a spot where we see the '*Torre del Oro*,' the famous tower of gold (a Moorish outwork or fortification); and the Guadalquivir winding for miles through olive-groves, and away towards Cadiz among the cork-trees.

From '*La Giralda*' we can also take a distant view of the 'Plaza de Toros,' and see the performance and the multitude without being present at its horrors. Across the river is the rather disreputable suburb called Triana, inhabited by a race of gipsies, who live in a half-Arab fashion, conforming as little as possible to Spanish habits.

It is the very place for picturesque old buildings, and for painters who wish to study the costumes and habits of the gipsies of Andalusia.

Two other features on the map beneath are the wide Campo Santo—the playground of Seville; and one enormous building, in itself almost a town, the tobacco manufactory, covering a quadrangle of 600 feet, where about 4000 persons are constantly employed.

Seville is situated in a flat country, with nothing remarkably pretty or attractive about it, on the banks of a narrow river with anything but a 'crystal bosom,' on which there are some barges, and a small steamer sending out volumes of smoke. Its streets are badly paved, and the roads in the environs are almost impassable after rain.

From the tower of St. Mark's at Venice the view is somewhat similar, but there is nothing here to compare with the '*Canale Grande*' and the broad lagunes; and we cannot, in whatever direction we look, discern much that is imposing, either in the situation or the buildings of Seville.

If in the twelfth century it was one of the most considerable cities in Spain, it is still the most favoured spot; the fertility of the soil and the beauty of the climate, rendering it at all times a desirable residence. The capital of a province, with a population, in 1861, of about 118,000, it is a town of great importance; and when we have visited its chief places of interest, and mixed more amongst its people, we shall, perhaps, alter our tone a little, and acknowledge the truth of the Spanish proverb, '*Quien non ha visto à Sevilla, no ha visto à maravilla.*'

The Cathedral is in itself a 'wonder:' and we should have thought that no history of 'Gothic Architecture in Spain' could have been complete without including this edifice.

The interior is sombre and blocked with the 'coro,' and it takes some minutes before one can appreciate its real extent. The ground-plan is enormous, 400 feet by 260 feet. It is divided into seven naves, the centre being 134 feet in height; thirty-six pillars support the roof, each 15 feet in diameter, and 'around them are grouped shafts, slender, thin, and light, like so many reeds around an oak-trunk, terminating in slender palm-branches, blending gently with each other.'

> 'Bound with leaf garlands tender, rise stately and slender
> The great massive pillars.' . . . .

On our first visit we were conducted in a dreamy manner through upwards of thirty chapels.

We were shown the splendours of the 'retablo' of the high altar; the 'coro,' with its statues of 'prophets, priests, and kings;' and the 'capilla real,' with its tombs and arabesques.

We passed on to examine the most remarkable of ninety-three painted glass windows, and, as well as the dim light would permit, Murillo's famous picture of 'St. Anthony' and other *chefs d'œuvre* of this master. The variety and beauty of the objects in the chapels, especially the 'sacristia mayor' with its 'pomp of marble,' would occupy a volume to describe and weeks to comprehend.

But the chief delight of a visit to the cathedral at Seville—after having seen about a quarter of what is set down by the 'cicerone'—is to go alone towards evening, when vespers are sung and the great organ is sometimes played, and to see the effect of the interior almost in darkness, whilst streams of light shine through the painted windows above.

Coming out through the beautiful 'Puerta del Puerdon,' a remnant of the ancient mosque, into the 'Court of Oranges,' we see the 'Giralda,' with its fretted arabesque ornament glowing in the last rays of the sun, and are again, in imagination, in the land of the Moors.

Seville is the birthplace of Murillo, and

the *Caridad* (a hospital and church in one) contains some of his finest works. Here is the great picture of the 'Miracle of the Loaves and Fishes,' and opposite to it 'Moses in the Wilderness.' They are well hung, but rather too high for close examination. Murillo's treatment of these subjects is well known by the numerous engravings and copies: the originals are in excellent preservation, and enable us to appreciate his greatness as a colourist, as much as we had already done (from Esteve's engraving) his wonderful skill in composition and grouping.

There are several smaller works by the same master. The most celebrated are the 'St. John the Baptist' and the 'Infant Saviour,' which are set in panels, each over an altar. Let us not forget to notice his '*San Juan de Dios*,' 'St. John with an angel'—a magnificent work; and let us avoid, if possible, Valdés' abomination, a large picture of a prelate in a state of decomposition, to which guides invariably first conduct the visitor.

At the Museo, which is open free on Sundays and fête days, but to see which we were obliged to obtain a special permission from the director, a separate room is set apart for the Murillos.

There is one picture here of which we must

speak, Murillo's '*Santa Tomas de Villanueva*' (No. 155), which exhibits his skill and power more than any picture we have ever seen. The calm natural dignity of the prelate giving alms to a kneeling beggar; a woman on the left hand with her child, who is showing the money it has just received, and in the foreground one of those beggar-boys that Murillo delighted to paint—every figure being a study of character from life.

There were other Spanish painters represented, including valuable works by Zurburan and Valdés, and one or two most successful examples of *painted* sculpture; one figure especially, St. Dominick of Montañes, carved in wood, has a startling effect of reality.

Some of our party made a pilgrimage to the house where (it is believed) Murillo died, now inhabited by the dean, Don Manuel Cepero, who has done all in his power to preserve the remains of ancient art which still grace the city of Seville, and who has saved many of the Murillos from destruction. His house is situated near the city wall, and the dean is very courteous to strangers and glad to show his collection of paintings.

There were two Moorish edifices yet to be seen, the 'Alcazar' and 'Pilate's House.'

The Alcazar is part of a Moorish palace, rebuilt by 'Pedro the Cruel' in 1353, with the aid of architects from the Alhambra. From the cathedral tower we noticed traces of the original extent of this building, reaching to the 'Torre del Oro' on the river side, and in several other directions. It has been added to at several periods and in different styles of architecture. The Hall of the Ambassadors is a splendid saloon, with four vestibules and Moorish arches, very rich in decoration.

Some of the rooms are spoilt by modern work, and in this hall there are several portraits of Spanish kings, which are completely out of place and ruin the effect. We approach the rooms through a patio surrounded by 'azuelos'—one of the most beautiful apartments is the 'Sala de Justicia.'

The restorations in these courts have been executed with little taste, and the gilding and painting have been applied without care or the requisite knowledge of colour.[1] Nothing speaks more highly of the manner in which Mr. Owen Jones's decorations at Sydenham have been exe-

---

[1] It is well to take our first impression of Moorish decoration from Seville, for after seeing the 'Alhambra' at Granada we could not admire this.

cuted than by contrasting them with the 'Alcazar' at Seville—both being reproductions of the same alhambraic work.

We were conducted through several suites of rooms, some of them leading out into gardens. These gardens must have been the delight of the inhabitants in the palmy days of Seville. Here are orange and lemon trees laden with fruit, myrtles and cypresses, flowers and rare exotic plants. There are *perforated* marble walks, which at a given signal send up hundreds of little jets of water to cool the air and refresh the ground, besides curious baths and other buildings which we cannot detail, and which are nearly all associated with tales of cruelty and horror in the time of 'Pedro the Cruel.' These stories are dinned into the unwilling ears of visitors by the guides. Here 'one fair lady was tortured;' there another 'was put to a lingering death;' 'observe the stains of blood on the marble pavement,' &c.; in fact, we almost recoil from the mention of the place.

The other Moorish building that we visited was the *Casa de Pilato*, which is said to be like Pontius Pilate's house at Jerusalem. In parts of the interior it resembles the Alcazar, although of course much smaller. There is a beautiful patio paved with marble, with a fountain ornamented with dolphins, and statues of goddesses at the four angles. There are several handsome apartments and a magnificent staircase leading to a gallery. From the terrace-roof there is a good view over the city and into the now neglected gardens, giving a good idea of the 'housetops' of the East, and the general character of the buildings at Jerusalem.

We have spoken of the chief sights of Seville; let us now make one or two extracts from our note-book about our stay at the 'Fonda de Paris,' and the style of living. 'The company that we meet is more select than at Madrid, but we cannot say much for their manners. A Spanish countess, with her suite, who monopolises all the best rooms in the hotel, makes her appearance, with her family, at dinner. It is ungallant to say it, but she is coarse and illmannered, and offends against every canon of good taste. Her children smoke at table, scramble for the different dishes, and carry off the dessert in their hands. Greediness and a grovelling style of getting through meals are the chief characteristics of the Spanish portion of our company. A general officer, who sits near us every day, has lately come to Seville for the benefit of his health, and this is his method of taking care of himself. For breakfast he commences with a huge lump of Dutch cheese and a plateful of hard unripe pears. He takes five or six tumblers of cold water, besides as many sour apples as he can get within his reach. At dinner, between the courses, he beguiles his time by again devouring hard apples, radishes, olives, plums, and sponge-cakes, 'ad libitum.' We have now witnessed this terrible performance for so many days that we cannot help making a note of it.'

'The ordinary diet is nearly as poor as in Castile: there is no good beef or mutton,—the latter being considered poor food, sheep are never properly fed for the market: the pork is better, but '*toujours porc*' is worse than '*toujours perdrix*.' Game and wild fowl—in fact, any bird, beast, or fish that feeds itself—is the best in Spain. The fowls sent to table have been so thoroughly boiled before roasting, that they are beyond the pale of criticism. One of the best dishes is composed of rice, pimentoes, cockles (including sand and shells), well boiled in oily gravy. There is no fresh butter, but bread and chocolate are excellent as usual. The native wines have a strong unpleasant flavour. We like the sherry, but not its price, 9s. or 10s. a bottle, and we are only a few miles from Jerez!'

But are we sure that we have seen Seville—the Seville that we are to 'see and die'—the capital of Andalusia, the seat of refinement and learning, the chosen home of the αριστοι of the south of Spain?

If in Madrid politics are uppermost in men's minds—if in Cadiz or Barcelona commerce is of the most importance—in Seville they give place to poetry, music, and the '*belles lettres.*' Let us, as far as time will permit, endeavour to penetrate its mysteries, and take a peep at its inner life and domestic society.

Fortified with letters of introduction, we will go to one or two of the first houses on our list, and, without particularising, sketch their general aspect as they strike a stranger.

Passing down almost any street in Seville, the senses are gratified with the most delightful perfumes issuing from the inner patios, and with sounds of music and dancing. Enter, by a door of open metal-work, through a hall paved with marble, into the inner court, filled with plants and flowers; a fountain is playing in the centre, and an awning overhangs, which keeps the air cool all the day long. There, with such 'surroundings' as tropical plants, sculpture, antique hanging lamps, and prettily tiled walls, the Sevillians spend their

lives in their summer drawing-rooms, and in their cosy little 'boudoirs' leading on to balconies, of which we just get a peep here and there.

All the principal rooms lead on to the central court, where visitors are received, concerts are held, and the main business of life is transacted; varying, of course, very much according to the position, or taste, or wealth of the owner. Everything has such an air of home comfort and luxury about it, that we, in our insular ignorance, are quite taken by surprise. Here at least is one continental nation that understands the meaning of the word 'comfort,' and can appreciate 'home.'

But Seville is not itself without '*life*'—life in music, in dance, in song—animation everywhere.

Mr. Lundgren, who spent years in this city and has studied and sketched Seville in all its phases, has given us in this illustration a picture of life in the middle class. The patio is smaller than those we have just spoken of: it is more open to the street, and the scene is more homely, but the spirit is the same, and the group gives an excellent idea of the prevailing style of feature and indoor costume. Of the Spanish dances we shall have to speak more particularly at Granada.

Of course all this has its reverse. You may

enter the next patio and find it a perfect bear-garden—a chaos of disorder. Another perhaps is neglected and in ruin, and then it looks desolate indeed. The aloes have grown and stretched out their sharp-pointed leaves almost to bar your entrance, vine-branches are trailing on the ground, palm-trees bend mournfully down, and the air seems oppressed with an over-growth.

Would that we had had time to do Seville justice and to stay during the summer months, for, as Lady Tenison observes, the style of living of which we have spoken is 'peculiar to Seville and to Seville alone;' but it is only in summer that it is seen to advantage, for 'patio life ends in September and does not recommence until May.'

It is to be regretted that many of our countrymen pass through Seville without a glimpse at all this. They take no introductions to residents, and content themselves with 'doing the lions' and departing. If they see a dance, it is generally at the theatre, or a got-up affair by two or three second-rate ballet-dancers in a room near the hotels.

A word or two about their domestic architecture. The Spaniards, we know, are greatly indebted to the Moors for their admirable method of building—a method which we believe is more applicable to houses in our own climate than is generally supposed.

When we consider that the average lives of women and children who dwell in cities are spent almost as much within four walls as the figures in the child's toy of Noah and his family in the ark, which are taken out once or twice a day to be looked at and then shut up again, one would think that the study of the fitness and beauty of our Noah's arks would be more considered. It is altogether an error to suppose that the climate is the secret of the difference—it has something to do with it, but not much. They have fogs and damp, continual rain and cold, driving winds at Seville and Granada at certain seasons, when protection from the weather is the first necessity; but the Moors surmounted the difficulty, and these dwellings, now used and copied by Spaniards, are suitable both for heat and cold.

We venture to suggest that, in many particulars, such as in the proportion and arrangement of the different rooms, their height, the shapes of their doors and windows, their system of ventilation, and their freedom from draughts, they offer valuable hints to builders, if not to architects.

Perfection in these arrangements we shall see at Granada, and there alone.

The Bullfights here are so notorious that the visitor feels that he has not seen Seville until he has 'assisted' at one of the performances. But, as we hinted at Madrid, centralization is rapidly doing its work all over Spain, and even bull-fighters come within its influence. The programme is the same, but the performances are shabbier and conducted with less spirit than formerly, and the crowd is more unruly than at Madrid.

We will not repeat a description of an ordinary bullfight, which will be found in a previous chapter, but shortly describe a burlesque upon it, which took place at Seville during our stay, on one of the red-letter days of the Church's calendar, for the benefit of 'certain masses, and other acts of piety and charity.'

We take the following from our notes nearly verbatim, leaving out the worst details, and must be pardoned if, in the enthusiasm of the moment, we seem to have entered too much into the spirit of the sport. Parts of the performance were disgusting, and quite unfit to be witnessed by any English lady.

The great attraction of the day was the first appearance of an 'intrepid *señorita*'—'tauromaniac' we should be disposed to call her—who was to face the bull singlehanded. This drew crowds of spectators; and when the ring was cleared, and the young lady entered, in a kind of 'bloomer' costume, with a cap and red spangled tunic, the audience rose to welcome her. She bowed to the president, and was conducted at once into the centre of the arena, when lo! a great tub, with one end open, was brought and placed upright and the 'intrepid' lifted into it! It reached to her armpits, and there she stood waving her 'banderillas' or darts, when at a given signal the bull was let in. It was a young bull, with horns cut short and padded at the ends; and as the animal could only toss or do any mischief by *lowering* its head to the ground, the risk did not seem great or the performance promising.

For some time the bull would not have anything to do with the tub, evidently not considering it fair game, but after walking two or three times round the arena he turned round suddenly, and without the slightest warning rushed headlong at it. Away went the tub, rolling half across the arena, with our fair señorita, who had evidently rehearsed her part, coiled up inside.

This was all very well, and the lady might enjoy a sport usually confined to the hedgehog and other lower animals; but when the bull, who soon began to get angry, at last caught up the barrel on his horns, and rushed bellowing round the ring, it looked serious for the tenant. There was a general rush of 'banderillos' and 'chulos' to the rescue, but some minutes elapsed before they could surround the bull and rescue the performer from her perilous position. When extricated she was smuggled ignominiously out of the arena, and we saw the brave *señorita* no more: the bull was not killed, but 'bundled' out of the ring.

The next act was 'Skittles.' Nine negroes ('Bedouins of the desert' we should call them in England), dressed grotesquely, stood up like 'ninepins,' within a few feet of each other, and a frisky '*novillado*,' or young bull, was let in to knock them over. They understood their duty, and went down flat at the first charge. The bull struck out right and left, and soon overturned them all. They then sat in rows in chairs, and were again bowled over, to the delight of the assembly. This was great fun, and was repeated several times—the bull liked it, the 'ninepins' *seemed* to like it, and the people gloried in it.

The third act was a burlesque of the 'picadores;' a grotesque but a sadder sight. Five poor men in rags, who, for the sake of two or three reales, allowed themselves to be mounted on donkeys and receive the charge of the bull.

We could not help thinking that it was not alone Cervantes who had 'laughed Spain's chivalry away,' if the stately Sevillians could enjoy such sights as these.

'But we must not stay to moralise, the sight is too ridiculous. Here they come in close phalanx, cheered by at least 5000 people; the five donkeys with their ears well forward, and their tails set closely between their legs; the ragged 'picadores,' without saddle or bridle, riding with a jaunty air, and a grim smile on their dirty faces, that was comical in the extreme. Would that Gustave Doré could have seen the group!

The gates are opened again, and the bull goes to work. He charges them at once, but they are so closely packed that they resist the shock and the bull retires. He has broken one of the poor animal's legs, but they tie it up with a handkerchief, and continue marching slowly round, keeping well together as their only chance. A few more charges and down they all go. The men run for their lives and leap the barriers, and the donkeys are thrown up in the air!

Such is a general outline of the performance, which had many variations and interludes, and lasted more than three hours.

As evening approached the whole scene made one of those pictures that delight an artist. The 'Plaza de Toros,' at Seville, is half in ruins; one side of the wall being destroyed, and through this gap we saw the city. The foreground was an irregular mass of people, scarce distinguishable in the twilight, but twinkling with the light of thousands of 'cigaritos,' and covered with a complete canopy of smoke floating in the still air. Beyond, the city towers just tinged with the sun's departing rays, and 'La Giralda,' high above them all, glowing as if it were yet broad day.

The finale was a wonderful sight. Two or three young bulls were let into the ring, and then *all the people*. We left them there, rolling and tumbling over one another in the darkness, shouting and screaming, fighting and cursing—sending up sounds that might indeed make angels weep.

CHAPTER XI.

CADIZ—MALAGA.

FROM Seville to Cadiz by railway is a slow and easy journey of about five hours, passing no objects of great interest until we reach Jerez, the residence of many of our countrymen, and the chief town in the wine-producing districts of Andalusia. It is a bright and pleasant-looking place, with a cathedral and 'alcazar,' and several enormous structures dedicated to Bacchus, its patron saint.

Those who intend to visit one of the 'bodegas,' or wine-stores, will be glad to know that in Jerez, 'inns are middling; wine, as bad as can be expected in a wine-producing country, and dearer than in London!'

Soon after leaving Jerez we begin to get glimpses of the blue sea, and the beautiful Bay of Cadiz, which stretches for miles in a southerly direction. Vessels, displaying the colours of various nations, are riding at anchor, and the town glistens and sparkles in the sunshine, looking as if it were an island far out at sea, situated as it is on the extreme point of a narrow neck of land. We can see it, as we travel by the railway, for fully an hour before we arrive at the port.

As we approach the port, a number of people enter the carriage which we have previously had entirely to ourselves. There are English, French, Germans, and Spaniards, and we hear our own language spoken almost for the first time since we entered Spain.

The difference in style and manners between the people of Seville and the more brusque and busy inhabitants of Cadiz and its neighbourhood must strike the most superficial observer. The distinction is certainly not imaginary, although the old nobility, both of Cordova and Seville, may be considered a 'thought' too proud and exclusive.

Seville—stately in her people, stately in her dwellings—looks down upon the commercial city of Cadiz with the same proper pride and serene content with which the inhabitants of our good old city of Bath contemplate Bristol and its flourishing trade.[1] Watered by the same rivers,

---

[1] We might carry the analogy a step further, and suggest, as an illustration of the size and general arrangement of a Spanish bull-ring, that the 'Circus' at Bath would make an admirable 'Plaza de Toros,' with an unexampled view from its front windows!

connected by railway, and in continual communication, their inhabitants preserve their own characteristics, and cling to a distinction that it would be sometimes difficult to define.

Charming—bewitching are the girls of Cadiz, with a beauty which roused Byron to something like enthusiasm, and, in later times, inspired Hans Andersen to sing:—

> 'Like a rose she is so fresh and sweet—
> A living rose, in which red and white meet.
> Before me she shines like the mountain's snow;
> In her eyes the tints of the heaven glow.
> A houri she is, yet a fiend in heart—
> Delightful, yet acting a demon's part.
> She gazes at me with her sparkling eyes;
> Before those warm glances all prudence flies.'
> * * * *

And to conclude with a rhapsody that we have not space for, by appealing to the 'unimpassioned daughter of the north' in these words:—

> 'O northern lotus, say a prayer for one
> Enthrall'd amidst these daughters of the sun!'

Charming as indeed they are, with their lustrous eyes and long lashes, luxuriant hair and bright complexions, they are not, as we said, comparable to the Sevillians. Their features are not as good, and there is not the same refinement or delicacy of expression.

The young men of Cadiz, over-dressed in modern costume, with a profusion of rings, and a partiality for fancy umbrellas, have not to our insular eyes either the dignity or the repose of the well-bred European.

But one thing we notice to our comfort in travelling in this part of Spain — we are not jostled and treated with quite so much indifference or contempt. 'The young dandy that has been sending his stream of tobacco-smoke straight across the carriage for the last three hours, until we are becoming gradually 'cured,' is quite effeminate in his politeness, in the interest he seems to take in our welfare, and in the anxiety he expresses that we should take a 'cigarito.'

'The dark girl with him, wearing a mantilla, and a bright red camellia in her hair, quietly dressed in black, is amiability itself, and her not very regular features are beaming with expression and goodness; indeed we have never seen, before or since, so much expression on any face in complete repose.'

The town of Cadiz, at which we have arrived whilst we are criticising our fellow-travellers, almost dazzles us with its brightness on emerging from the railway station (which is close to the harbour, and near to the centre of the town):

we might be in an eastern city, but that the port looks more like a miniature Marseilles.

Cadiz is splendidly situated, at a considerable elevation, and with the sea on both sides. From its position, and its importance as a trading port, it is a populous thriving place, possessing a strong military garrison. The long, narrow streets are clean and well kept; the houses are high, many of them handsome, with a magnificent sea view; they are nearly all whitewashed and plain in exterior, relieved by bright-green shutters and coloured blinds and awnings. There is a pleasant 'Alameda' facing the sea, but the most favourite promenade is on the fortifications near the port— the great place on summer evenings to see the beauties of Cadiz.

We walked at once to the '*Fonda de Paris*,' where we had friends awaiting us; it is centrally situated, comfortable, and nearly as dear as Madrid. We found very little to do besides walking about the town and watching the people.

The best view of the city is from the sea: and there is not a more pleasant excursion in fine weather than to sail across the beautiful bay of Cadiz to Santa Maria, near the mouth of the Guadalquivir. It is possible still to go to Seville by water, but the railway has thrown this route into disuse; the old steamer, the last time we saw it, was piled up ten feet above the deck with salt fish and other merchandise, and little room was left for passengers.

For once (and the discovery was perhaps rather a relief) there were no public buildings, 'museos,' or cathedrals, that we were bound to visit. We were free to lounge about on the sea-shore, or go to the market-place and sketch the groups composed of different nationalities and costumes. It reminded us of the '*Place*' at Algiers, to see negroes and Arabs carrying enormous baskets of oriental-looking fruits, to hear a perfect 'Babel' of sounds, and to see the bright minarets with their flagstaffs, with a background of deep-blue sky, and broad expanse of sea.

In the old shops there were trinkets from Tangiers and Malta, filigree work, oriental stuffs and silks; and in others the celebrated Cadiz kid gloves were to be purchased at less than one franc a pair. They are strong, and look well at a distance, but the workmanship is very rough; and we were informed, on the best authority, that they were not worth the trouble of bringing home.

Cadiz ought to be a healthy town; but we

could not help remarking during our stay that we hardly ever went abroad without seeing a funeral. A procession of boys with lighted candles, a priest followed by four bearers half hidden under a pall, hurrying through the least frequented streets, was a sight that we soon became accustomed to, and which seemed scarcely heeded by the inhabitants.

It was 'only the Cadiz fever,' the Spaniards said, and no doubt it was true; but it takes time to be acclimatised to anything; and when your courier or servant suddenly disappears and dies in a few hours (as happened to us at Seville), and another steps into his place without a word of explanation, a feeling comes over you that your own particular existence is of less importance in Spain, and that, if illness overtook you in this land, you must not expect much concern to be expressed, or much notice to be taken of it.

If a traveller alone, is taken ill at an inn, he has not much chance; Spaniards will sell him medicine, and send him a priest if he will have him; but if he get worse and be on the point of death, they will make very little excitement about it. It is 'the will of God,'—the Moslem creed of passive non-resistance and no-trouble-taking, finding favour with Spaniards on all such emergencies,

—they submit to fate; smuggling the body out of the hotel at dead of night, and throwing it into a pit outside the city. Excepting at Madrid, Malaga, and Cadiz, where there are English residents, and where Protestant burial-grounds have lately been established, it goes hard with the stranger who ends his days in Spain.

The traveller, whether by land or by sea, must on all occasions 'look after' himself, and see to the security of the vehicles he intrusts himself to. To be turned out of a '*lartana*' (a curious kind of high gig peculiar to the south of Spain, eccentrically painted, and bearing some resemblance to those used in England thirty years ago); to experience 'shaves' when an overladen and rickety diligence is careering down hill; to meet two or three young bulls in a narrow street followed by a hundred delighted boys,—are merely '*Cosas de España*,' and part of the fun of the country; but when it comes to drowning it is more serious.

On the walls of Cadiz there were advertisements of steamers plying between this port and Gibraltar, Malaga, and Tangiers. One evening in the autumn of 1864, a fellow traveller who was desirous of taking a passage in one of them, applied at the agent's office, and was informed that he was 'just too late,' that the berths were taken, and that he must wait for the next steamer. That little vessel steamed out of the harbour on the following morning, with her crew, passengers, and cargo, and disappeared like a myth; from that day to this no tidings of her have ever been heard. It was *supposed* that her cargo had shifted during a gale, and that she had gone to the bottom.

What happened when she did not arrive at her destination? Nothing.

What happened when, days and weeks afterwards, friends and relatives of those on board besieged the steam-packet offices for some tidings or clue to her disappearance? Nothing.

What happened when, weeks afterwards, a list of the passengers was published in the Madrid '*Correspondencia*'? Nothing.

It was 'the will of Allah,' and so the company put another vessel on the station. Facts are indeed stranger than fiction, but let us hope that this was an exceptional case, and that with an increase of traffic there will be better steamers between these ports. We speak of things as we found them in 1864!

We decided upon going direct to Malaga, and secured berths several days beforehand in one of Lopez and Co.'s steamers, which leave

Cadiz every Friday afternoon. It was lying half a mile from the shore, for no other reason that we could imagine (there being plenty of water to come in) than to provide a comfortable income to the *marineros*, who carry on business on the same principles as our well-beloved Dover boatmen of old time. There was a '*tarif*'—there always is a '*tarif*'—but it was of no avail. What it cost us for luggage alone, to transport two portmanteaus from the '*Fonda de Paris*' into the hold of the steamer, the reader, who has not been troubled with many statistics, may like to see by the following; which does not include 'black mail' levied by the beggars *en route*.

'Valet de place'[1]—to secure 'a good boat and trusty boatmen'—one dollar . .	20 rs.
Porterage, for getting the portmanteaus down stairs into the patio . .	4 rs.
Assistant, and cord to tie them together .	4 rs.
Porter (who carried *four* enormous trunks and several portmanteaus on his back down to the port) for our share .	8 rs.
Getting them into the boat (our share) .	4 rs.
,, ,, out of the boat (,,) .	4 rs.
Boat	6 rs.
	50 rs.

[1] The 'valet de place' was almost a necessity to enable us to get off in time. We had generally considered couriers and 'valets de place' little better than a nuisance until we came to this country, when we soon found out their value.

The luggage came to about 10s. 6d., without including our fares to the boatmen, which were nearly as much again. If we had contested the matter and fought our way inch by inch, we should probably have saved some 'reales,' and—been disturbed in mind for the rest of the day.

The weather had been stormy, and the white crests of waves which we could just see outside the harbour, and the driving clouds, did not look very promising. However, the voyage was a good one; we left Cadiz at 3.30 P.M., and arrived at Malaga at six on the following morning.

About 10 P.M. we passed through the Straits of Gibraltar; it was moonlight, and we could see 'the Rock,' and the lights, both on this shore and at Tangiers.

We lay off Malaga for nearly two hours, waiting for the opening of the Custom-house: and the coast and distant range of the Sierra Nevada were just becoming tinged with the rays of the morning sun, when the gun fired, and we entered the harbour. The wind had gone down, but there was a considerable ground-swell which made landing in small boats rather difficult. Directly the first person stepped into one of the little boats he disappeared, and seemed to sink into the waves, and the next went up into the air, and so on. Landing at the quay was no easy matter, and getting through the Custom-house to our hotel on the 'Alameda,' a work of time and a trial of patience.

Malaga subsists on its export trade, and is a very busy place. The principal features of the town, as seen from the sea, are the cathedral and the old fortress on the heights; the houses are white and plainly built. Its population is about one hundred thousand, the greater portion of whom are engaged in commerce; in nearly every other house and in the open street they are to be seen busy packing oranges, lemons, and raisins, for exportation.

The 'Alameda,' the chief public walk, is planted with acacia-trees, and decorated with a marble fountain. It is situated between two rows of houses, and is hot and dusty in summer, and muddy in winter; but it is not much frequented excepting on Sundays.

We had heard that this town was famed for the beauty of the women, but they did not seem to us nearly as attractive as those at Cadiz. They have fine eyes and teeth, and luxuriant hair; and as long as they continue to wear the mantilla with fresh flowers in their hair, they cannot but be attractive. Lady Tenison was disappointed with the 'almost total absence of beauty amongst Spanish women,' but thought that the Malagueñas were 'entitled to dispute the palm with the inhabitants of any other city.'

We saw more English faces here than at Cadiz, and the appearance of the town, the habits of the people,—everything, gave evidence that its inhabitants were accustomed to English visitors. At the ' Fonda de la Alameda' we were made very comfortable, and could have boarded for the winter for five or six shillings a day.

The English people seemed to be the only idlers, excepting the beggars. As for the latter, directly we set foot in the street they came round us in such numbers (praying, blessing, and cursing, according to their humour), so brown, so ragged, so dry and parched, that they looked as if a spark from one of their own *cigaritos* would have set them all in a blaze.

Such a wretched crowd it has rarely been our lot to encounter. In any other climate they must have been taken to the hospital or the 'casual ward' of a workhouse; but here, nature is so bountiful, that, with an almost perpetual summer, with figs, oranges, dates, &c., growing wild, no one can starve: they can only—we must borrow the word —'moon' their lives away.

As for the middle class—the shopkeepers—their nonchalance was most amusing. We went into a confectioner's one day to purchase some chocolate, and were deliberately told that, if we liked to get it down from a high shelf, we could have it; no assistance was offered, and we had to go empty away. In another place, we had been selecting some photographs and prints, and suddenly found that we had not time to conclude our purchase that day. Never shall we forget the air of relief with which the man shut up the portfolios and lighted his *cigarito*. If we would but leave him in peace, and come 'mañaña,' he would be ever grateful.

If the 'laisser aller' theory seems to be carried a little too far when they have to earn their daily bread, it is at any rate refreshing to mix with a people with whom money-getting is not the 'summum bonum' or the important business of their lives.

The Spaniards are temperate and dignified, but they are also very cruel. Nothing strikes a stranger more, than their want of pity for the sufferings of animals. Here, for instance, as we sit on the 'Alameda,' we see little birds, tied by a string to a stick, sold as toys to children, who throw them about alive and drag them in the mud. Horses and other animals are treated with great neglect and cruelty, and the sufferings of animals only seem to be considered, when they are likely to affect the value of the living commodity.

With regard to the climate of Malaga, and without questioning the wisdom of prescribing the air here for some constitutions (see Dr. Lee's 'Spain and its Climates'), we can only say that we found it, in winter, very damp and enervating. The principal streets were nearly a foot deep in soft mud: from the sea, and from the hills above, the town had often the appearance of being in a vapour-bath; and in the dry season the dust is very disagreeable. We believe that Madeira is far preferable as a winter residence, although the drives in the neighbourhood of Malaga, and by the sea, are delightful: the mean temperature of the latter is 55·41 in winter.[1]

On Sunday we attended the English service at the Consul's house, which was held in a large chamber appropriated to the purpose: we also went to the cathedral, and to the English cemetery, from which there is a glorious view of the bay.

From our window on the Alameda we had

[1] See O'Shea's Guide to Spain. p. 319.

noticed, for the last two days, an object which appeared to be the ruins of an omnibus or diligence, and had, we had observed, been temporarily converted into a fowl-house. It lay over on one side, so dilapidated and mud-bespattered that its outline was hardly distinguishable, and it was a matter of wonderment to us how it ever got on to the Alameda, and why it was not pulled down and carted away.

On the afternoon of our departure from Malaga we heard a noise of hammering and carpentering, and saw a crowd of idlers assembled round this structure. A beggar, who had been sleeping inside, was unearthed, and sundry chains and implements were thrown out into the road. All this we were watching with a languid curiosity, when it was suddenly heightened by seeing a team of mules attached, and by being informed that this was our conveyance to Granada, and to be our residence, until seven o'clock on the following morning.

Much ingenuity and fertility of resource were exhibited in converting this rickety vehicle into a 'moveable body.' The chains by which the traces were held, were cunningly attached to the hinder, as well as to the fore-part, of the carriage, and the whole so bound and corded (with our portmanteaus on the top), that—given sufficient draught-power, it *must* go. How it was to be extricated from its muddy bed, in which it lay 'canting' over, with two wheels half-hidden, was not our business. All we had to do was to squeeze into the little 'berlina,' amongst the straw and dirt, and set to work to endeavour to manufacture out of paper, or our pocket-handkerchiefs, some sort of window or shutter to keep out the night air.

'*Arré, arré — macho — macho-o!*' — with a struggle and a crash, our crazy conveyance lunged out of its hole, and, being nearly empty, was suddenly as lively and frisky as the proverbial tin kettle tied to a dog's tail, and which, in its eccentric evolutions, it now resembled. How it held together at all, under such treatment, was, and always will be, a mystery. The driver and 'mayoral' sat with their backs against the open space where windows had once been, and held on as they best could; and thus, to the sound of cracking of whips and the shouting of the driver, we rattled, and bumped, and plunged through the streets, and were soon out in the open country.

The diligences on this road are said to be 'the dearest in Europe,' and, judging from the accommodation, we began to believe it.

Our party having divided for a time, we were now only two in number, and the only passengers by the diligence. After ascending for about three hours, we came suddenly upon a scene of splendour that no pen could ever describe, and few pencils have successfully handled. It was one of those sunsets with which we have been made familiar in paintings by Danby or Vacher, but which we seldom have the good fortune to see in nature.

We had reached a height of nearly 3000 feet, and the bay of Malaga was spread out beneath us like a map. We could almost trace the coastline to St. Roque and the African shore. The sun was setting behind the mountains, and shedding a glorious light across the bay; in the middle distance a slight veil of mist rose from the valley, and, as it rose, took a warm purple half-tone—subtle and delicate. The foreground was almost in darkness, and the giant forms of aloes and cacti stood out in bold relief against the sky, with just sufficient reflected light to bring out the variety and sharpness of their outlines. Immediately above our heads the stars were shining, and on our left the moon was reflected in the still water. As a picture it was far finer than an eastern sunset, from the variety of atmospheric effect and the incomparable beauty of the coast.

We were tempted to do our utmost to bring this scene before the reader in an illustration, but it would have been a failure without colour: we thought it better to substitute a drawing of the colossal vegetation in the neighbourhood of Malaga, detailed from a photograph with as much minuteness as the scale would permit.

Would that we could prevail upon our landscape-painters who have sketched Italy and Sicily so often, to come to Spain! With its buildings and its people we are all familiar, but the glory of its landscape is to most of us unknown.

When night came on, and we had reached the highest parts of the lonely and bleak Sierras, the warm air was succeeded by blasts of cold icy wind, that penetrated our frail tenement, whistled through its crevices, and howled through the open windows. At one point, where there was some difficulty about a relay of mules, and we were left alone for about an hour, without driver or team, on an exposed part of the road, the wind beat against the vehicle with a violence that nearly lifted it from its wheels, and made every timber groan.

Time was, not long ago, when two travellers, unarmed, could hardly have passed securely in the night across the desolate slopes of the Sierra Nevada; but there was no need of fear here; we were much more concerned about keeping out the wind, and as to whether our 'rattletrap' conveyance would hold together through the night. It had one chance against the hurricane—there were so many holes and open windows that the force of the wind was lost by passing *through* the vehicle.

Twelve years ago the best, safest, and quickest way of performing the journey from Malaga to Granada was to hire mules. There were then no diligences, and the *galeras* were too slow and too rough a mode of conveyance to be agreeable. Artists have reason to regret the gradual disuse of *galeras* as subjects for their pencil. They were covered carts without springs, drawn sometimes by one mule, sometimes by eight or ten; they corresponded to our old-fashioned market carts, and were generally crowded with people and things innumerable, festooned on the outside with animals and birds, alive and dead, and piled up with fruit and merchandise. Their midday halt at the 'posada' has often been brought before us on canvas.

But as we are anxious to get to Granada, we are thankful to O'Donnell's system of 'Guardias Civiles,' that has made the roads more secure, and caused the establishment of regular conveyances of a somewhat better and quicker description.

After another instalment of jolting, during which we just manage to doze, and to go through several acts of a hideous nightmare, in which we are the most important of the *dramatis personæ*; we are suddenly awakened with a crashing noise, and by being suddenly thrown against the front of the carriage. It was not exactly a breakdown, for we had arrived at the town of Loja; the driver had only made a slight miscalculation, and sent us banging against the door-step of the old 'posada.'

It was two o'clock in the morning, and we were glad to enter the little inn and warm ourselves. There were several figures lying about on the floor asleep; an old woman roused herself and made some chocolate, and then all sat round the 'brazero' for half an hour. Before we left, the company began to increase in number, and the effect of the quaint group round the fire, with the rest of the interior in darkness, and the stars shining through an opening overhead, made another picture to be remembered.

We were soon again in the open country, and, when it dawned, had nearly reached our destination. Granada was before us; and above the town 'there rose, as it were, another city, called—"*Alhamrā*." '

CHAPTER XII.

GRANADA.

'The gardens of thy Vega, its fields and blooming bowers —
Woe, woe! I see their beauty gone, and scatter'd all their flowers'

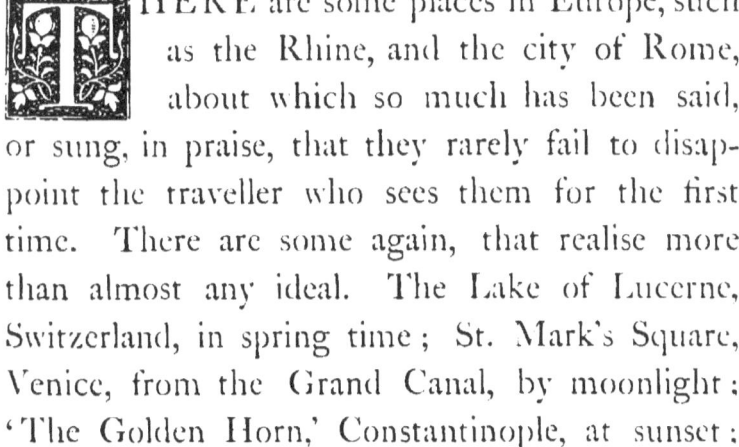HERE are some places in Europe, such as the Rhine, and the city of Rome, about which so much has been said, or sung, in praise, that they rarely fail to disappoint the traveller who sees them for the first time. There are some again, that realise more than almost any ideal. The Lake of Lucerne, Switzerland, in spring time; St. Mark's Square, Venice, from the Grand Canal, by moonlight; 'The Golden Horn,' Constantinople, at sunset; and—at all times and seasons—Granada.

Whether it be from association, or the romantic beauty of the situation, everything seems to combine to satisfy the spectator. Artist, poet, philosopher, antiquary (or mere holiday lounger, who may be all or none of these), will each find something to his mind, and each, according to his taste and temper, *must* be more or less gratified.

Our illustration is taken from the garden of the 'Generaliffe,' which is situated on the heights above the Alhambra, from which it is separated by a deep ravine; we can see a portion of the town and the plains beyond, and it enables us to form some idea of the general plan of the palace itself. We can trace the old walls and towers for a considerable distance—the latter were formerly the residences of the sultanas and their families, and still bear traces of magnificent decoration. We can see the conical roofs of the 'Court of Lions,' and the great square building erected by Charles V., to build which a portion of the Moorish palace was removed.

It is evident from this drawing what a splendid situation the Moors selected to build upon, and what noble views they must have had from their windows over the Vega, thirty miles in extent. We see the town below, the rows of stately elms, the luxuriant gardens, and the cornfields beyond; but even here, the pride and great glory of Granada we cannot see—the snow-capped mountains of the Sierra Nevada, which

rise in the opposite direction, and form of themselves a perfect picture of alpine beauty.[1]

Here at least, at Granada, we can live quietly and enjoy ourselves. There is a little inn built into a part of the old walls of the Alhambra, called the '*Fonda de los Siete Suelos*,' which is well adapted for an artist, and in summer, for any one staying for a length of time.[2]

This '*Fonda*' is nearly half a mile from the town, up a steep ascent, and, although a 'perfect place' in summer, and for work; we could hardly recommend it as convenient for a short visit. It has, of course, the advantage of the moonlight walks on the terraces, but in winter (we must be matter-of-fact sometimes) it is damp, and extremely inconvenient to return to after dark; and you lose much that is to be seen in the town itself in the evening. We stayed at the '*Fonda del Alameda*,' on the Alameda; a comfortable and well-ordered inn, kept by a Piedmontese, a very civil and obliging host.

---

[1] In a former work we endeavoured to direct attention to the Atlas mountains in Algeria as 'new ground' for Alpine travellers. We have not explored the higher ranges of the Sierra Nevada, but they appear to offer a still finer field for research.

[2] This inn has lately been sold; travellers now stay at the '*Fonda de Ortiz*,' also situated near to the Alhambra (April, 1866).

After a good night's rest, and considerable study of 'Murray,' perhaps the best way to see the sights of Granada is to engage the services of a guide by the day, as you are not allowed, without special permission, to visit the Alhambra alone. E. Bensaken (*père*), the same guide who assisted Ford and Owen Jones in their labours, is to be heard of at this hotel, and seems tolerably well qualified to speak of the Alhambra. His information is not always accurate, but he knows more about the place than any other local guide. He had an especial attraction for us, because he had Moorish sympathies, and told his story of the ruin and degradation of the place with an earnestness that was partly genuine. It was like a voice from the dead—'the last wail of the banished Moor.'

Bensaken is a 'character.' Born at Gibraltar, of Moorish parents, he was brought up as a money-changer; and afterwards served under the Count Montijo (uncle of the present Empress of France), whilst Captain-General of Granada, until he was put into the Inquisition in 1817. Of late years he has acted as chief guide and interpreter at Granada, and has had the privilege of showing many royal personages over these buildings, our Prince of Wales amongst the number. He has printed a short account of Granada, which he sells to travellers; but it is better to draw him out, and hear him talk.

Early on the first morning after our arrival, we set off to visit the apartments of the Alhambra. Fighting our way through the crowd of beggars, who lay in wait for our coming, we pass up some steep and irregularly paved streets, and under a massive archway built in the time of Charles V., and are immediately within the precincts of the Alhambra. We walk up long avenues, planted on either side with tall elms, between which we catch glimpses of the red towers far above us, and soon arrive at the 'Gate of Justice,' with its horseshoe arch, and marble pillars, and the superscription—

'There is no power or strength but in Allah.'

Thence by a path between high walls to a large open terrace, called 'The Place of the Cisterns,' commanding a fine view of the surrounding country; past the palace of Charles V. (the prominent building in our illustration), to a little mean-looking door in one corner of the square, and are, without being aware of it, within six yards of the chief object of our pilgrimage.

Our credentials being examined, we are at once conducted through the 'Patio de la Alberca,' or the 'Court of the Fishponds,' an oblong court, with a sheet of water in which are reflected the slender columns of a portico, rich with moresque decoration.

A few paces further, at the end of a corridor, the 'Court of Lions.' Its appearance was quite familiar — having been so often described, pictured, modelled, and copied, in part and in whole, there seemed as if there were nothing new to examine or discover; and we could not help comparing notes, in our mind, with Owen Jones's restorations, and mentally admiring the fidelity of his copy of this court.

But here we have the marks of time, the mellow tints of age upon the marble shafts and conical roofs, and the deep-blue sky overhead; and its proportions (so much larger than Mr. Owen Jones's model) give an effect of elegance and lightness for which we are unprepared. The court is grass-grown, and the fountain is dry. One side is under repair, and busy hands are at work *reproducing* (not restoring) what time and vandals have destroyed, or allowed to go to ruin. Some of the lace-like ornamentation is in wonderful preservation, and here and there we can trace the remains of the original colours with which this court was decorated.

The Court of Lions measures 100 feet by 50, and is surrounded by a portico supported by 144 marble columns, arranged irregularly. The variety and beauty of the ornamentation are seen almost to better advantage in the light-brown tint in which they now are, and it seemed to us that the whole aspect of this court could scarcely be improved by the addition of colour.

Leading from the Court of Lions is the 'Hall of the two Sisters,' with its beautiful stalactite roof, a 'profusion of vaults and miniature domes.' The walls are richly decorated and inscribed with sentences from the Koran:

'There is no conqueror but God,' &c. &c.

And on shields, several times repeated:

'God alone the conqueror.'

In this hall it would seem as though the skill of Moorish artizans had been exerted to the utmost; the most precious woods and marbles, the rarest mosaics, and the most delicate carvings and sculpture having been employed to embellish it.

On the opposite side of the Court of Lions, and also leading out of it, is the 'Court of the Abencerrages,' and at the end, the Hall of Justice.

But what seemed to us most admirable was

the 'Hall of Ambassadors.' Its noble proportions (37 feet square by 75 feet high), its position, the views from its arched windows over the distant country, and also into the 'Court of the Fishpond,' with its flowers, seen through another corridor: the recesses in the windows, the proportion of every door and window, and the delicacy of the decorative work, interlaced, as usual, with inscriptions and praises to God.

We were shown the Baths—a suite of luxurious apartments, with a central patio or 'chamber of rest,' which is at present under repair, and is being richly 'restored' in colour; also other chambers and the *Mosque*.

But time, and Charles V.'s furniture and whitewash, when he turned it into a chapel, have obliterated nearly all the Moorish work, although the ceiling is very fine. In this chamber we were shown a beautiful recess where the Koran was kept.

In the first visit to the Alhambra it is difficult to see and remember much more than we have indicated (for you are not permitted to stay long in one apartment), but after two or three visits the eye becomes accustomed to the style of architecture and decoration, and comprehends the intention and plan of many parts, of the building and ornamentation, which at first sight seemed confused.

TOWERS OF THE ALHAMBRA, BY MOONLIGHT

... ...
... ...
... ...

—WASHINGTON IRVING

So much injury has been done to the Alhambra by visitors, that the custodian is *not permitted to let any one remain within the walls unattended*, and, of course, prefers showing the rooms to a large party at a time—a tiresome and irksome regulation that takes away from the pleasure of contemplating quietly the beauties of the place. It was only after repeated application, and by representing that we were artists anxious to make studies of portions of the building, that we obtained permission to remain a few hours alone in any of the courts.

But what could we say? are we not marched and 'vergered' through Westminster Abbey on the same principle?

To ascend the Alhambra towers, and walk on its terraces, was the chief delight of our stay at Granada, and we have endeavoured to give, in the illustration, some idea of their effect by moonlight.

After some time has been spent in the study and examination of these ruins—a time ever to be remembered—we are naturally led to inquire what is the great charm about the works of the Moors,

---

[1] The little handbook to the 'Alhambra Court' at the Crystal Palace at Sydenham, gives a capital description of this building.

and about the Alhambra especially, which makes us love to linger within its walls?

In Castile—at Burgos, Segovia, and Toledo—we have seen some of the noblest examples of early Christian architecture; but if we are not mistaken, we have seen nothing, as striking in beauty and power, and assuredly nothing, that will leave such an impression on the mind in after years, as the 'Alhambra.'

No doubt sentiment and association have much to do with this; but we believe that, to the unlearned in styles of architecture, the principles on which the Moors worked appeal more directly to the mind.

Simplicity, refinement, and truth are their chief characteristics. Looking at the severe exteriors of their towers and walls, giving no indication of the art, and luxury, and grace, that they concealed, we cannot admire too much the completeness of the general plan. Their palaces were formed, as Owen Jones remarks, 'like those of the ancient Egyptians, to impress the beholder with respect for the power and majesty of the king; whilst within, the fragrant flowers and running streams, the porcelain mosaics and gilded halls, were constantly made to remind the owner how all that ministered to his happiness was the gift of God.'

In decoration, both in form and colour, they worked on fixed principles. Owen Jones's analysis of their method of colouring has become well known in England since the Exhibition of 1851, and we can here judge for ourselves how valuable and true his teaching is. What he says about 'form' cannot be too often repeated :—

'A still further charm is found in the works of the Arabs and Moors from their conventional treatment of ornament, which, forbidden as they were by their creed to represent living forms, they carried to the highest perfection. They ever worked as Nature worked, but always avoided a direct transcript; they took her principles, but did not, as we do, attempt to copy her works. In this again they do not stand alone ; in every period of faith in art, all ornamentation was ennobled by the ideal; never was the sense of propriety violated by a too faithful representation of nature.'

In our illustrations we have given hardly any examples of Moorish work, not from want of abundance of material, but because the public has of late years been made not only very familiar with it, but, as some think, has seen and heard too much in praise of this style of architecture. We must, however, give one illustration of a portion of a door in the '*Patio de la Mesquita*,' because it seems to us to illustrate, so much better than any words, at once the delicacy, strength, and beauty of Moorish ornament.

This doorway is an admirable example of suggested strength and fitness, combined with variety, and appropriateness of design.

We were unable to do justice to the decoration on so small a scale; but it has been carefully engraved from a photograph, and enough indicated to give an idea of its general character.

The upper portion is a good example of relief work *without* colouring: the lower part, on each side, is white tiling, the patterns upon it being in blue, yellow, and black. At the capitals of the marble pillars may be observed portions of texts from the Koran, and it is interesting to notice how beautifully the cuneiform inscriptions blend with the other parts of the decoration.

We spoke of the general principles on which the Moors worked, and of their being forbidden by their creed to copy or to represent any living thing;[1] but they have, in this instance, approached very closely to an imitation of nature, in the introduction of the form of a shell into the ornamentation.

Many of the passages inscribed on the walls of the Alhambra are very appropriate and suggestive. In the 'Hall of the two Sisters' there is a sentence that runs thus:

'Look attentively at my elegance, and thou wilt reap the advantage of a commentary on decoration.'

And we may be sure that this would never have been written if the architects had not felt that, in so doing, they were not sounding their own praises,

---

[1] The lions supporting the central fountain in the 'Court of Lions,' were made *purposely* unnatural, on the same principle.

but evolving a principle, for there never was a nation that worked in all they did on truer principles: whatever they believed it right to do, they did it with their might.[1]

When we look at the arrangement of the halls and chambers of the Alhambra, with separate apartments for each of the Sultanas; and think of the sumptuous accommodation provided for them, and indeed for every member of the enormous retinue of the Palace, will it be thought unpatriotic, or very wrong, to compare it, for one instant, with the interior arrangements of our own palaces in the sixteenth century?

Is it not chronicled somewhere that in the reign of 'good Queen Bess' the maids of honour had to petition to 'have their chambers ceiled, and the partition that was of boards, to be made higher, for that the servants looked over;' and that the chamber for the squires of the body was so 'ruinous and cold,' that they begged to have it 'ceiled overhead and boarded under foot' to make it habitable?

---

[1] It is beyond the scope of this little work to enter into further details of Moorish architecture; but we cannot refrain from noticing how, in some modern dwellings (and, notably, in the decoration of the new 'Whitehall Club,' in London), the Moorish system of mural decoration seems to be finding favour in England, in 1866.

But whatever be thought of Moorish architects, judged by the standard of other nations, may we not attribute, at least a part, of their great success to the fact that they were *artists* as well as architects; that their education comprised a knowledge of engineering, of chemistry, of painting, and indeed of everything that was directly or indirectly applicable to their art?

They had moreover one great advantage over architects of our own day—they had nothing to unlearn. They knew their materials, and had not to endeavour, after a laborious and expensive education in one school, to modify and alter their method of treatment, to meet the exigencies of another. They were not 'cramped for space' or for money; they were not 'tied for time,' and were generally allowed to carry out their own plans.

'*Nov.* 8, 1864.—A lovely morning, though still cold. We went with Bensaken to see the remains of the ancient Seraglio, which is situated in a narrow street in the middle of the town. There is a Moorish gateway and a large shabby courtyard, with rooms all round, now occupied by poor people, who pay about 6*d.* a week for what were once apartments in a palace!

'Near it was the old bazaar, with open shops

under arcades with horseshoe arches, ornamented with Moorish patterns and supported by marble pillars. A few were tenanted, just sufficiently to give an idea of its former appearance when filled with gay costumes, rich silks, and embroideries.

'We also went to see the "Cartuja," a convent of Carthusian monks. It possesses little of its former wealth, having been completely plundered by the French; but they could not take away the wealth of marble, jasper, and onyx; or the doors inlaid with silver, ebony, and mother of pearl. It is now a mere show-place, stripped of half its treasures, but with enough remaining on its walls and doors to give an indication, that in the sanctuary especially, the architects must have aimed at repeating the glories of Solomon's Temple.

'In the refectory, a large empty chamber, there is a cross painted on the white wall to imitate real woodwork. It is executed so well that it is said 'birds fly in and attempt to perch upon it.' We had read about this and knew it was a painting, but were surprised to see, as we thought, a real nail fixed into the wall. The nail and its shadow proved to be more wonderfully painted still.'

It is useful, and saves much time to have

a 'cicerone' to conduct you over these buildings; and also to inspire the beggars with awe when exploring the town at night. The latter is sometimes almost necessary, for they infest Granada to such an extent that a stranger is often surrounded and literally stopped by them. These are not the gipsies, but a lawless mob of idlers, who stand at street-corners from morning until night, occasionally varying the monotony of their lives with a '*divertissement*' in the shape of a quarrel, or some act of plunder when their numbers are lessened.

But in spite of all we had heard of the wild character of the robbers and marauders of Spain, we may here mention that we hardly ever lost anything, or experienced intentional rudeness or violence; and only twice, saw the glitter of half-concealed knives which meant mischief.

In the mountains near Granada there is a primitive region where the inhabitants retain many of the habits and customs of the Moors; and in the suburb above the town (which we saw from the Generaliffe) there is a colony of gipsies who live in holes in the rock, hidden from the eye by a thickset plantation of cactus. They do not like intruders, but are glad enough to come down into the town and exhibit their national dances.

The captain of the band at Granada was a good musician; he played the violin and sang with great taste and skill. The dances were chiefly sustained by four young girls, dressed exactly as in our illustration, with abundance of bright colours and trinkets. One had a handsome Egyptian style of face, a clear dark complexion, black hair, fine eyes and teeth, and features most classically moulded; a face which, whether in animation or repose, was most striking.

The dancers stood up first in pairs, then all four together, and sometimes the men took part. They danced the '*bolero*' and '*fandangos*,' keeping time to quick music, and accompanying their movements by every variety of emotion expressed on their countenances. The national dances resemble those in the East, and depend almost entirely on the grace and expressive action of the performers, as there is no particular step, and few figures are attempted.

At one time the girls sang a monotonous chant, accompanied by the captain, on a guitar, and several pairs of castanets. As the song proceeded the expression on the girls' faces gradually became more and more animated, and the time was quickened, until the song culminated in a burst of joy that made the hills echo to the sound.

Another dance was expressive of fear, and several others followed indicative of other passions. Between the dances the girls came round and put one hand round the waist of each lady present, and, more cautiously, rested it for an instant on the shoulders of the other sex. It looked like a token of affection, but meant distinctly 'backshish.'

As there is hardly any one who has not read some account of the gipsies in Spain and their national dances, we will not detain the reader; but we should like just to draw his attention to the following little paragraph, culled from a newspaper last year, giving another traveller's description of these performances, which are certainly not 'straitlaced:'—

'The principal " bailarinas " were, a handsome, modest-looking young woman, of five or six and twenty, and a tall, strapping peasant-girl, a somewhat heavy-heeled Mænad, but possessed with a veritable fury for dancing. *El Zapatero* evidently knew his partners. With the first he behaved himself with the strictest propriety; the pair opening the ball with a slow and graceful " fandango," danced to a wild and plaintive tune, " as old as the hills "—" Chlodomir de Portugal " by name. This would have delighted the most fastidious beholder; but his performances with the other nymph were very different. With her, his demonstrations attained to such a pitch of Bacchanalian preposterousness, that I am afraid even the quaint and charming originality of " La cervera," " El fado," and one or two other very expressive

P

airs, the titles of which I could not catch, would not be held to counterbalance their unmistakable tendency.

'Thunders of applause—loudest at the most critical conjunctures—encouraged this lively cobbler and his unreserved partner; and I regret to say my impression was that the manners and customs of Moimenta were, at all events, not of the most straitlaced character.'

CHAPTER XIII.

GRANADA TO MADRID.

THERE is a choice of three routes homeward from Granada. The *first*, is to return to *Malaga* by Loja, and take the steamer to *Marseilles*. This is the easiest, and in many respects the pleasantest route in fine weather, and the descent upon Malaga is even finer than what we described when leaving it, in a previous chapter—surpassing anything on the cornice road between Genoa and Nice: then there is the view of the coast of Spain, with its background of snow-capped mountains, as seen from the deck of the steamer between Malaga and Barcelona. Alicante is not very interesting; but at Barcelona, where the steamers stop, a day, or two, may be spent very pleasantly. But the probability of bad weather in winter, and the excessive violence of the storms on this coast, changing a '*voyage de plaisir*' into a week's 'imprisonment, with a chance of being drowned,' must be taken into consideration.

The *second* route, is to ride on horseback by *Ronda* to *Gibraltar*, and take the English steamer to *Southampton*. This is tempting, because it takes us off the high roads, and we pass out of Spain by one of the most romantic rides in the world. There is nothing very difficult about it, even for ladies who are accustomed to the saddle. It takes four or five days to go to Gibraltar; and as numbers of travellers now pass this way, there is not much difficulty about obtaining good horses and tolerable accommodation on the road. The situation of Ronda itself, and some of the mountain defiles through which the path is carried, are wilder and grander in character than those of any other part of Spain; it is a favourite spot for artists, attracted both by the scenery and the costumes of the people. The following description is certainly not overdrawn.

'Ronda, containing about 24,000 inhabitants, is one of the most picturesquely situated cities in the world, and perfectly unique in its way.

'It is built on a very high rock, cleft in twain by volcanic action, and between whose precipitous sides or walls, flows the boiling Guadiaro, which girts the city, and takes here the name of Guadalvir, and divides the new city, *Ronda la Nueva,* from the older, *Ronda la Vieja.*

'On approaching this town from Granada, the country round is charming, valleys green and fresh. On the left, hills covered with the olive and the vine ; and on the right, well-cultivated fields, studded with pretty flat-roofed white cottages glittering in the sun, and the Sierra itself rising before one with its warm deep rich tints and bold outlines, greet the tourist.

'The streets of Ronda are clean, the rejas of the houses project into the street and contain quanties of flowers. The market-place *overhangs the chasm*. The Alameda commands an unrivalled view of the mountains, crowned by the lofty Cristabal. The view from the bridge over the Tajo, a grand and wild cascade of liquid silver, we do not attempt to describe—it baffles pen and pencil.'—*O'Shea*, p. 163.

The *third* route, by land, as indicated on the map, has many recommendations, and when the railways are completed will be the easiest. Returning to *Madrid*, we visit the cities of *Saragossa, Barcelona, Gerona, Perpignan,* and *Cette*, and leave Spain by its north-eastern shore.

We secured places for Madrid several days beforehand at the office of the '*Cordobesa.*' As the diligence portion of the journey was to take twenty-four hours, it was important to obtain places in the best carriages ; as, if the roads are heavy, they are apt to arrive late, and lose the only day train from Santa Cruz to Madrid, thus prolonging the journey through a second night.

The diligences on this road are 'the best

appointed in Spain,'—well-horsed, quick, and comfortable, and, if not very clean, they have at least windows that will shut, and are tolerably air and watertight. If two people take places in the 'berlina,' it is well worth while to 'compound' for the third place, or they will possibly have a 'middle-man' sleeping on their shoulders by turns all night. We have been under circumstances when this mode of passing the night has been endurable, if not pleasant; but in Spain the horrible reverse is much more probable.

These things may be thought too trivial for mention, but a good night's rest, or the want of it (with the addition of other things which we need not particularise), will just make the difference between a journey of pleasure and one of great fatigue and discomfort. When we travelled, the journey to Madrid took about thirty-four hours, twenty-four of which were passed in a diligence, with not an hour's halt on the road.

On the day we left Granada we walked down to the office on the Alameda at twelve o'clock, and waited amidst a crowd of idlers for the arrival of the diligence. It came up with a flourish, and much cracking of whips and blowing of horns, with a team of ten horses, gay with trappings and tassels. The diligence itself was painted bright yellow and red, and the whole equipage looked, outwardly, very pretty. The wheels wanted greasing, and the rope traces broke twice before starting; but these were minor matters, not worth a thought.

Of course we had to find out our places for ourselves. On opening the door of the 'berlina' the aspect of things was not cheerful. First of all there was a large dog coiled up asleep on the seat, a heap of rusty chain and old harness, and the driver's boots. The dirt was thick upon the cushions which lay at the bottom of the carriage, and the little den smelt—as it would be likely to smell, after having been shut up since the last passengers got out, and having since served as a bedroom for the 'mayoral' or the postboy. There was nothing for it but to make the best use of the ten minutes before starting, and 'turn to' and dust out our prison, turning out the dog, and the boots, and the harness, and giving the cushions a good beating against the wheels, before an admiring crowd of the concentrated idleness and dirt of the town, assembled on the 'Alameda' to see the start.

In the west of Ireland we have seen 'gentlemen' doing nothing, standing all day in a row, in the rain, in *dress coats* (somewhat ragged and brown it is true, and short in the tails), and were apt to think that this particular form of 'lounger' was peculiar to Great Britain. But our 'pisantry' are industrious and clean compared with the Andalusians. One is reminded of Murillo at every turn; his dirty boys, as pictured in the Dulwich Gallery, are to be seen here, fighting at the street-corner—ragged, unkempt, wolfish— very 'full of life' indeed.

We went off as usual with a rush, the team starting at once into a gallop, jingling, rattling, and crashing through the narrow streets, driving every foot-passenger into the nearest archway for refuge, jolting over roads, half-paving half-mudhole; out into the suburbs, where we sunk deep into mire, and swayed from side to side like a ship. On, by the banks of the river Darro, winding up into the mountains, where we looked down for the last time upon the plain of Andalusia; and, keeping up a good pace all day, arrived, soon after dusk, at *Jaen*. The scenery was wild, especially near the 'Puerta de Arenas,' where there is a long tunnel cut through the rock; but the road was good, and we passed too quickly to see it to advantage.

The moon was just rising as we approached Jaen, and we could understand how much we missed by not taking this journey leisurely on

horseback, and spending some days in the town and its neighbourhood. Jaen contains many curious buildings, and a fine cathedral in the 'Græco-Roman' style: its population is about 23,000. The streets are narrow and picturesque-looking.

If the author of 'Bridle Roads in Spain' ever sees these lines, he may smile at our saying that the accommodation at Jaen is bad, that the best '*Fonda*' is dirty and not too salubrious, that the character of the people is wild and reckless, and that the suburbs and neighbourhood are not too secure for moonlight walks. But as we are not in search of adventures, and are writing for ordinary English travellers who may come after us, it is as well to state the facts. Robberies still occur (the diligence was stopped near Bailen about a month ago), and the whole of this mountain-district gives great trouble to the authorities.

Mr. Lundgren, who knows the country well, has here given us a sketch of a group of natives, who may be plotting, or may not: we should think they were, and that there was not an honest man amongst the seven.

The designs that we have engraved for the ornamental headings to the chapters are taken from the embroidered patterns on the 'mantas,' worn as seen in this illustration.

As we pass out through the gates of Jaen into the open country we see the tall forms of the '*Guardias Civiles*' in their long cloaks, standing two and two, by the road-side, at intervals of a few miles, looking more like gaunt spectres haunting these windy sierras, than human beings; and we cannot wonder if, as it is *said*, as soon as the diligence has passed, they disappear to some place of refuge. Nothing would seem more dreary than to stand all through the night on the open plains, swept by a pitiless wind, without a tree or a shrub for shelter.

We had had several relays of horses and mules, when, a little before midnight, we stopped to change, at a place where a bridge was being constructed across a river at a great elevation. The cross timbers were only temporarily laid down, and there were no balustrades; yet it was already made use of by the diligence to save a *détour* of some miles.

The next stage was to be a fast one, and our weary team of mules was here changed for ten active, wild-looking little horses, which were led out and harnessed by the aid of (what seemed to our sleepy imagination) the whole population of the place. It turned out that it was quite necessary to have assistance to lead them quietly over the bridge, for the horses were fresh and restive, and the slightest accident would have overturned us into the river beneath.

We had scarcely crossed when the signal was given to 'let go.' The horses' 'heads were given to them,' a few stones thrown at the fractious ones, shouts and kicks, blessings and curses, and away we went. Two of the team had already got their hind legs over the traces, and another had his head out of his harness; but it was too late to stop. The pace was tremendous, and the sleepy travellers in the coupé above were rolled from side to side with a motion truly grand.

They travel fast in Russia, and we are accustomed to be proud of the speed of our stage-coaches in England; but not even the 'Wonder' or the 'Rocket,' no '*Malleposte*' or '*Correo*,' ever flew across country, as in that wild moonlight ride between Jaen and Bailen. The way before us was nearly flat, and the road hardly distinguishable (indeed, we lost it once or twice); nothing to be seen in front but the steaming backs, and heads, and gay trappings, of ten madly-tearing horses, just discernible by the lamp above; nothing to be heard but the rattle of the vehicle and the jingling of bells. We could just make out, once or twice, something at the road-side, –a tree, or a *patrole*, or a hut it might have been,—but it was out of sight in an instant. If there had been anything in our road, any accidental obstruction, we must have gone over it (or *through* it, as the Scotch limited mail did one night through a luggage-train that was crossing the line). Nothing could have stopped our horses suddenly; they had no bits or reins, and were simply running wild. Everything depended upon our postilion, who rode the leader, and was quietly peeling and eating apples all night!

The speed was well kept up until, at about 2 A.M., we arrived at Bailen, and joined other diligences on their way from Cordova to Santa Cruz. We were glad to stay here half an hour, and to get some delicious chocolate and biscuits at the old hostelry.

At twelve at noon we reached Santa Cruz, and rested at the wretched ' *Venta* ' until the train left, about two P.M. Our fellow-traveller to Madrid was an English engineer, who possessed a railway key, and, for once, we managed to get a compartment to ourselves, and to arrive at Madrid (at ten P.M.) without discomfort. We drove to the ' *Hôtel de Paris*,' on the ' Puerta del Sol,' and were glad enough to find ourselves once more in comfortable quarters.

On this, our second visit to Madrid, the cold was intense, and the wind piercing. We were struck with the incongruity of the women wearing fur boas and large muffs, with only a piece of thin net upon their heads; whilst the men were literally wrapped up to their eyes, having no other feature visible.

The sun shone brightly all day, and on the sunny side of the 'Puerta del Sol' the people came to warm themselves in its rays. The price of fuel was enormous, the wood that was supplied to us would not burn, and perhaps it was just as well that the fire went out so often, as the logs cost about sixpence apiece!

One more pleasant visit to the 'Museo;' another, to the wretched 'Correo' for letters, and we bid farewell to Madrid. As we cross the 'Puerta del Sol' for the last time, the familiar trumpet is heard from the barracks, and a closed carriage, with six mules, goes gaily by with the Royal infants, 'baptised with water from the river Jordan,' and 'christened with a hundred names.'

CHAPTER XIV.

MADRID—BARCELONA—PERPIGNAN.

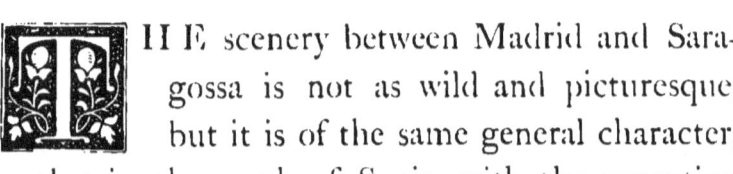HE scenery between Madrid and Saragossa is not as wild and picturesque, but it is of the same general character, as that in the north of Spain, with the exception that there are more rivers, and that here and there, on emerging from a tunnel, or on winding round a mountain, we come into a pleasant watered valley, which reminds us of Andalusia. Artists stop at Guadalajara, and at Siguenza, which, like Jaen, are full of interest; the old buildings, narrow streets, and quaint local costumes of these towns, and also of Cuenca, are made familiar to us in picture galleries in England. In all these places accommodation for travellers is, of course, rough, but not worse than in many other 'out-of-the-way' spots in Europe.

The journey as far as Saragossa is so wearisome, that we have recommended travellers, in the

Appendix, to leave Madrid at night. There are many reasons for this; you escape the dust and *heat*, and there is not much to see *en passant*. At night the Spaniard sleeps, and we would rather have him snore, than make himself otherwise unpleasant when awake. Again, the trains are quicker at night, and there is less probability of any 'accident' or delay.[1]

Some friends were detained several hours on this line on their way to Madrid, in October, 1865, owing to what the officials called an 'accident,' but which turned out to be one of those very common occurrences in this part of Spain, a popular *émeute*. The suppression of all intelligence of the cause of the delay was so well managed by the Government and the railway employés, that our friends knew nothing of what had occurred until they read the following, in a newspaper at Madrid, several days afterwards.

'*Tumults at Saragossa, Oct.* 4, 1865.—Particulars have been received here of the disturbances at Saragossa on the 2nd and 3rd inst., which, at first quietly suppressed, broke out a second time, necessitating the action of the military, and resulting in loss of life amongst the rioters. The disturbance originated in the refusal of the peasants to pay the octroi upon provisions entering the city. The demonstration

---

[1] It is perhaps better (as we did) not to make any stay at Saragossa on the homeward journey.

commenced on the morning of the 2nd inst., when many peasants refused payment of the tax at the gates, and others collected in groups, assuming a hostile attitude towards the authorities.

'On the morning of the 3rd inst., however, the demonstrations of the peasants became more serious. They assembled at the gates of the city, and impeded not only the entry of provisions but the passage of travellers proceeding to the railway stations. The civil authority, after vainly endeavouring to persuade them to disperse quietly, left the conduct of affairs in the hands of the Captain-General Don Juan Lapatero, who, following instructions received from the Government, published a notice giving the multitude one hour to disperse. At the expiration of this time the Captain-General headed his troops and made a charge to clear the streets, when the peopled fled and dispersed. At four o'clock in the afternoon all was quiet, and it was hoped that public tranquillity had been restored. At eight, however, those concerned in the disturbances of the morning again formed a tumultuous assemblage in the streets. The military were immediately on the spot, and, on receiving a shower of stones from the mob, fired two or three times in the air to intimidate the rioters. To this the peasants replied by a fresh volley of stones and some discharges of firearms. The troops then fired upon them, killing and wounding several of the peasantry, and order was then restored.'[1]

This is a fair illustration of what is continually happening in Spain, and which gives the charm of uncertainty to all one's movements.

---

[1] The military at Saragossa were thus spoken of in the official report of the recent revolts in Spain: 'The attitude of the garrison of Saragossa is as admirable as it is energetic, and is a model of discipline against the revolution.'

The traveller who has just arrived at Madrid from the south, who has perhaps escaped quarantine at Gibraltar, Cadiz, or Barcelona; who has visited Ronda on horseback, or crossed the Sierra Morena by diligence, with no more than the average number of small '*contretemps*' and delays, is apt to congratulate himself that he is once more on a railway, and to feel that now at least he may calculate upon arriving at his destination at the time proposed. But in Spain, railways are as liable to be delayed, and to break down altogether, as almost any other mode of conveyance. The peculiar nature of the country, so liable to storms and floods, the bad state of the rails, and the general carelessness of the people, combine to render their '*Indicador del Ferro Carril*' little better than a 'delusion and a snare.'

Had we gone to Valencia in November, 1864, we should have found the railway washed away in several places by the floods, and all communication with the interior interrupted.

Had we attempted to leave Madrid by the northern or southern lines in October, 1865 (when the cholera was so much dreaded), we should have found the termini besieged by a panic-stricken mob, who waited outside day and night until they could gain admittance. In two or three weeks, 80,000 people left Madrid by its two railways, their ordinary passenger traffic not averaging more than two or three hundred a day.

While we are writing (January, 1866), news comes from the south that a number of travellers are detained on the Sierra Morena, and cannot pass the lines of General Prim's troops; that the railway is torn up at Tembleque, and communication is once more stopped with the south.

In about an hour and a half after leaving Saragossa we arrive at Tardienta, the most northern point on our journey to Barcelona. We are now only about sixty miles from Jaca, and three days' journey, riding and walking, from Luchon, in the French Pyrenees. Very few people enter Spain by this route, on account of the want of good accommodation, and the difficulty of obtaining any information beforehand, but it is at once the most direct and picturesque approach to Spain.

At Huesca (the seat of the ancient kings of Aragon), about nine miles north of Tardienta, on the route just mentioned, and at Lerida, a station on this railway at which we arrive in six hours after leaving Saragossa, the antiquary will find many objects of interest. Mr. Street says that 'such a cathedral as that of Lerida is alone worth the journey from England to see;' but, he adds (what we heard *en route*), that 'its examination is beset with difficulties, if, indeed, it will be allowed at all, when visitors become more numerous than they have been hitherto.'

In a few hours we reach Manresa, and, leaving the plains of Aragon, the railway winds amongst the hills, keeping in sight of the Montserrat range of mountains for many miles; and in about two hours more we arrive at Barcelona.

The crush at this station, and the turmoil before we reach our hotel, '*De las Cuatros Naciones*,' on the 'Rambla,' are matters of course.

Barcelona, the capital of Catalonia, has been called the Paris of Spain, but we should be more disposed to compare it to Liverpool. It is a great commercial port, strongly fortified, and contains nearly 200,000 inhabitants. The first time we ever saw this city was from the sea, in coming from the Balearic islands, and it certainly looked to greater advantage than when approached by land. But directly we enter its gates we see plenty of signs of gaiety, prosperity, and commercial activity; the fine modern buildings, cafés, and promenades, giving an appearance of life and gaiety that we were beginning to think was not possible in Spain.

'La Rambla,' which is parallel to the seashore, is the great promenade of Barcelona, and is crowded in the evening, when the cafés are lighted up, and sounds of music and dancing issue from the houses and public gardens. Everybody meets on the Rambla, where half the town is congregated on summer evenings.

The harbour is filled with ships of all nations, and the port crowded with their wares. The traveller who is on his homeward journey, will probably not stay long after having visited the cathedral, and one or two of the principal churches; nor is there much to be bought that is peculiar to Barcelona, unless perhaps a few of the trinkets and silver ornaments, which used to be one of the special manufactures of the city, and are still worn by the peasantry. The goldsmiths' and jewellers' shops are amongst the most interesting sights in Barcelona.

But the genial climate, the sea-breezes, the walks by the shore, and the drives to the hills (where the wealthier Barcelonese have pretty villas), render it at all times attractive for a stay or a residence.[1]

There are two railways to Gerona, which is reached in about three hours. The country through which we pass, on the inland route, is green and fertile, tropical in its vegetation, and bright-looking from the number of little villages which are interspersed amongst the hills; but the line by the sea is more generally taken.

The ordinary rapid mode of travelling, and the difficulties thrown in the way of stopping *en route*, when taking tickets at Barcelona to Perpignan, carry many a traveller too quickly through the quaint old city of Gerona. Situated on the banks of the Oña, once the centre of a considerable trade and commerce with France, it stands now desolate and deserted-looking to a rapid observer, but the artist and antiquary will be well rewarded by a closer examination. Its present population is about 1400. There is a fine Gothic cathedral, which has a history,[2] and

---

[1] 'The temperature of Barcelona is very mild. it snows seldom, and the heat in summer never exceeds 31° Cent, nor falls below 2 under zero.'—*O'Shea.*

[2] 'Gothic Architecture in Spain.' p. 318.

which dates from the time that the Moors held possession, although the exterior is not imposing. Mr. Street gives a long account of its architectural details, and an illustration of the curious high altar made of silver; and of 'a pretty example of a wheel of bells,' such as we have noticed in other churches in Spain.

The '*Fonda de la Estrella*,' at which we stay, is one of several curious old buildings scattered over the town.

The railway ends at Gerona, and we are soon again in a comparatively barren and mountainous district, with here and there a poor village and an oasis of cultivation. The roads are generally good, and, excepting in the rainy season, when the torrent-beds are full, and streams have to be forded at full speed, there is little material for excitement on the road, excepting the natural one, that we are galloping out of Spain as fast as eight good horses can take us. Diligences have been overturned, and they have been stopped by robbers, between Gerona and Perpignan; but such occurrences are too rare to be thought of, and there is now almost perfect security on this road. Nevertheless, from what we know of this land, we should not care to wander much amongst the mountains alone after dusk, unless well armed or in the costume of the country.

In a few hours we descend into half-cultivated plains, planted with olive and cork trees, and rattle through the streets of the old town of Figueras, with its strongly-garrisoned citadel and arsenal, and where there are about 20,000 troops to 7000 other inhabitants!

A beautiful ride over the '*Col de Pertús*' brings us once more into France, being about twelve hours from Gerona to Perpignan.

Here our Spanish journey is at an end; but although we have crossed the frontier, we are still amongst a people with strong Spanish sympathies. The inhabitants of both sides of the Pyrenees were formerly like one nation; and at this time, there is no part of Spain which pulsates more quickly and truly with the heart of the nation than the '*chef lieu des Pyrenées Orientales*.' The news of the last insurrection (January 1866) had scarcely reached Paris and London when news came that Perpignan had risen, that 'shots had been fired at the crowds assembled,' and that some persons had been killed and wounded.

CHAPTER XV.

CONCLUSION.

THERE are one or two points to notice before concluding.

In keeping to the high roads, so much is missed that ought to be seen, and so much is seen that it were better never to have encountered, that we would strongly recommend every one not tied for time, and possessing the least knowledge of Spanish, to break through the routine as often as possible; or at least to follow one or two of the bridle-roads, now approached by railway for the first time.

Such, for instance, as to enter Spain over the Pyrenees by the *Port de Venasque*, or through the Province of Andorre; or to journey from Pau and *Eaux Chaudes* to Jaca and Huesca, joining the railway at Almudevar, on the line between Saragossa and Barcelona, and leaving it again at Siguenza or Guadalajara; thence continuing by diligence, or on mules, to Cuenca.

From Cuenca it is possible to go south, either towards Andalusia or Valencia.

Then the ride from Granada to Ronda, or Granada to Murcia, halting at wayside posadas, and camping on the mountains. There is little or no personal risk in these excursions, and the cost is of course much less than on ordinary routes.

Although we took a different course, travelled by first-class conveyances, went to the best hotels we could find, and sometimes passed rapidly through the country, it was from circumstance and not from choice. We by no means recommend this to others, for there is but one way to see Spain—to live in the country, and to wander away from the high roads of modern civilization.

Artists and others of our countrymen who have spent years in Spain know well, that, for the sum we each expended in less than three months, they could live for a year, and that, in that year, they would probably experience less discomfort and meet with fewer rebuffs, than we did during a short visit.

Spain is not a country to travel in, and there is no nation which is more unfairly estimated, by foreigners, who pay it only a flying visit.

We have no opportunity of appreciating the

Spaniards' good points; nor do we become at all aware of their latent fund of humour, their good-heartedness, and their true '*bonhomie*.' We jostle with them in crowds, we rub roughly against them in travelling, our patience is sorely tried, and we are apt, as Miss Eyre did, to denounce them as worse than 'barbarians.' But we should bear in mind that Spaniards differ from other nations conspicuously in this—that they become sooner '*crystallized;*' and crystals, we all know well, are never seen to advantage when in contact with foreign bodies.

In short, Spaniards are not as other men; and Spain is a dear, delightful land of contraries, where nothing ever happens as you expect it, and where 'coming objects *never* cast their shadows before.'

The suggestion has often been made lately, that Spain was in a state of transition, and that it would be better for travellers to postpone their visits to this country for two or three years, on the ground that railways would then be completed to all the important towns, and that in many other respects, matters would go more smoothly; that Spaniards would be more accustomed to strangers and treat them with more consideration, and that bodily comforts would be better attended to, in the establishment of hotels, &c., by foreigners.

We believe that this, like every other promise, or hope, or prospect for Spain, will turn out to the contrary. 'Nothing but the unforeseen ever happens.' If we wait for the Spanish *mañana*, we shall delay too long. It will be too late to see any costume, excepting that of the poorest and most tawdry kind; too late to see the 'Alhambra,' which is disappearing under the hands of the 'restorer,' carefully though he works; and *too late* for, some at least of, the Spanish *railways!*

Will it be believed that they too, are disappearing fast? The line which was opened throughout, between Madrid and Cordova last year, now only reaches to Venta di Cardenas; and other lines, which have never been paid for, are gradually becoming dilapidated. We were assured by an engineer, who was at Barcelona at the beginning of the present year, that the 'permanent way' of one or two lines near that city, is positively unsafe and 'going to pieces,' for want of a few ordinary repairs—the proverbial 'stitch in time.'[1]

---

[1] There is no place in Europe, or perhaps even in America, where you may have the opportunity of seeing a locomotive more, what is technically called 'lively,' than on the lines near Barcelona.

Each year a visit to Spain is postponed, some of its characteristics will be lost. Costume is dying out — the cosmopolitan 'chimney-pot' carries everything before it; old buildings fall, or are destroyed, to make way for French warehouses. Everything becomes dearer, and wherever the tourist goes in 1870 he will find that Manchester has been there before him. The artist has not an hour to lose, and we believe there never was a better time, than this present year 1866, to visit the country, because now, for the first time, railways will take him rapidly to within a short distance of his destination, and they have not yet done for Spain what they will surely do—destroy its picturesqueness, and banish all chivalry out of the land.

CHAP. XV. *DETAILS OF THE ALHAMBRA.* 237

Architectural Details of the Alhambra.

[From the 'History of the Mahommedan Empire in Spain.']

GENERAL PLAN.

'SIMPLE and natural is the general distribution. The courts, for instance, which in our mansions are usually dull and uninteresting, are here so planned as to seem a continuation of the series of apartments; and the whole being upon a level plan throughout, in its primitive state the prospect must have been enchanting; halls and galleries, porticoes and columns, arches, mosaics, and balsamic plants and flowers of various hues, were seen through the haze of spraying fountains.

'Although the Arabs were unacquainted with perspective, yet their architectural scenery is truly picturesque, and well calculated to make a small building appear larger than it really is. Instead of the costly works of classic art, they adorned the courts and haram with the simple productions of nature, and blessed the God of Mahomet for having given them original pictures instead of copies.

'In every part of the palace they had water in abundance, and a perfect control over it; making it high or low, visible or invisible, at pleasure—sometimes spouting in the air, dispersing the floating miasmata, and tempering the aridity of the atmosphere. In every apartment two currents of air were constantly in motion, apertures being formed near the ceiling to discharge the warm and unwholesome air which the pure *inferior* current forced upwards. By means of tubes or caleducts of baked earth, placed in the walls, a subterraneous hypocaust diffused warmth, not only through the whole range of the baths, but to all the contiguous upper apartments where warmth was required.

'The doors are generally very large and sparingly introduced—except in the side towards the precipice, where the prospect is very grand; the windows are so placed as to confine the view to the interior of the palace.'

Ornamentation.

'The arabesques, paintings, and mosaics, which are finished with great care and accuracy, give a consequence and interest, even to the smallest apartment. Instead of being papered and wainscoted, the walls are covered with arabesques which had been cast in moulds in a peculiar manner, and afterwards joined together, although no separation appears. The receding ornaments are illuminated in just gradations with leaf-gold, pink, light blue, and dusky purple; the first colour is the nearest, the last the most distant from the eye, but the general surface is white.

'The domes and arcades are also formed of ornamented casts, which are almost as light as wood and as durable as marble. Specimens of the composition of which they are formed have been found unimpaired after a lapse of ten centuries. The art of rendering timber and paints durable, and of making porcelain, mosaics, arabesques, and other ornaments, began and ended in western Europe with the Arabs.'

Architectural Remains.

'The large cistern contiguous to the palace is a solid and durable structure, and the ingenious manner of filtering and keeping the water which is conveyed to it in the winter pure, and at the same temperature throughout the year, may deserve to be imitated, especially in tropical climates.

'Several matamoras or subterranean granaries still subsist in the eastern and highest part of the fortress. For the use of its inhabitants such a number of stores would not have been necessary; they seem sufficiently capacious to contain corn for the city of Granada at its most populous era.'

Statistics of Spain.

[From the 'Revue Contemporaine,' 1865.]

'It has been calculated that about the time of Julius Cæsar Spain must have contained 78,000,000 inhabitants, and yet in 1688 it did not contain more than 8,000,000.

'But from that time forward there has been a constant increase; in 1768 the population had risen to 9,307,800 souls; in 1789 to 10,061,480; in 1797 it exceeded 12,000,000 souls. In 1820 it had fallen to 11,000,000 or thereabouts; but in 1823 it had again risen to 12,000,000, and in 1828 to 13,698,029. Nevertheless, the official return of 1837 only registers 12,222,872 souls, and a new tendency to decrease commences. In 1842 the population was not found to exceed 12,054,000 souls. It rose again by about 110,000 in 1846, but fell again to 10,942,000 in 1850, if the official documents of the period may be credited; for in 1861 a census taken with the greatest care, shows the population to be about 16,000,000.

'When we consider that this number represents a population spread over a surface of 506,648 square kilometres, it is still far too thinly peopled. *Nearly 46 per cent. of the whole surface of the kingdom is still uncultivated.* Out of 3,803,991 able-bodied men, 125,000 belong to the clergy, 241,335 to the army, navy, and military functionaries, and 478,716 to the nobility. The remainder comprises 47,312 students, 5,673 advocates, 9,351 writers, 27,922 belonging to the customs, and 206,090 servants; forming a total of 1,221,799 men living apart from all manufacturing or agricultural labour.

'The export trade of Spain, which in 1849 was only 270,000,000f., rose in 1861 to 865,000,000f.'

Appendix.

CORRECTED TO APRIL, 1866.

The details in this Appendix refer chiefly to the Route marked (in red) on the Map, but they will be found to give information respecting *Distances*, *Times*, *Fares*, &c., between most of the important towns in Spain, both by land and sea.

The *Distances* are shown in English miles, and the *Fares* in both Spanish and English money. The Hours for starting of Railway trains, Diligences, and Steamboats, have been corrected to April, 1866.

Living at Hotels and incidental expenses averaged 15*s*. a day each person (without travelling), but this might have been considerably reduced.

The whole journey, as indicated on the map, may be accomplished in two, or three, months, but ought to take much longer. The expenses would average from 60*l*. to 90*l*. each person. According to other travellers, 50*l*. are 'ample' for this journey; but we did not find it so.

Paris to Madrid.—There is only one 'through-train' from Paris to Madrid, leaving *Paris* at 8·15 P.M.; arriving at *Bordeaux* at 7·5 A.M., *Irun* at 2 P.M., and *Madrid* at 10·40 A.M. Distance 900 miles. Fare;* Paris to Irun, 91frs. 20c.; Irun to Madrid, 278rs. 75c. (Through tickets, Paris to Madrid, about 6*l*. 11*s*. 6*d*.) Time, 36 hours in summer, and 40 in winter.

It is better to break the journey at *Bayonne* and *Burgos*.

BAYONNE. (Pop. 20,000.) *Hôtel St. Étienne; Hôtel du Commerce.*

Bayonne to Burgos.— Railway—Dep. 6 A.M. Arr. 5·46 P.M.
Distance, 193 miles. ,, 12·35 P.M. ,, 11·9 P.M.
Fares—Bayonne to Irun, 4f. 5c. } (Bayonne to Burgos, 28*s*.)
Irun to Burgos, 118rs.
Time, 10 to 12 hours.

---

* All fares are put down for 1st class on railways and 'Berlina' (*coupé*) diligence. For 2nd class, deduct about 20 per cent., or nearly one quarter. The population of towns is taken from 1861 Population Tables. The times of trains are corrected by the latest 'Indicador de los Caminos de Hierro,' published at Madrid.

The *only* 'quick train' (which averages about 20 miles an hour) is at 12·35 P.M., leaving *Biarritz* at 12·54, arriving at *Irun* at 1·45 P.M., where there is a delay of about an hour: all luggage is examined, and passengers have to *change carriages*.

Tickets may be taken at Bayonne or Biarritz for Burgos in French money; but it is necessary before crossing the frontier to be provided with plenty of Spanish money—gold or silver (not paper), which can generally be obtained at a banker's in Bayonne, or, if not, at *Hendaye*, on the frontier. This should not be put off until the last moment, as there is a scarcity of Spanish coin in France, and it will be found necessary before reaching Madrid.

If stopping at Burgos, the railway fare from that town to Madrid will have to be paid in Spanish money, and hotel-keepers will not exchange French 'Napoleons,' excepting at a great loss to the traveller.

Luggage is registered as in France; 30 kil. are allowed for each passenger.

At *Irun* it is advisable to buy (for 2 rs.) a copy of the '*Indicador de los Caminos de Hierro*,' the official railway guide, which, when we travelled, it was impossible to obtain in France. It is neither very clear nor very accurate, but it contains the best information on the subject, with a rough map of railways in Spain, some of which are not in existence.

The mail-train leaves *Irun* at 2·50 P.M., arrives at St. Sebastian at 3·23, at Alsasua* at 6·13, at *Miranda* (the junction with the Bilbao and Tudela Railway) at 8·2 P.M., and at 11·9 P.M. arrives at

BURGOS. (Pop. 25,000; alt. 2867 ft.) Hotels, none good: *Fonda del Norte* the best; *La Rafaela*, old and tolerable.

Luggage is examined here, as on entering nearly every large town or province in Spain; but the search is not strict, as the officials have an objection to the trouble of unstrapping portmanteaus, &c. If only making a short stay at Burgos, luggage may be left for a day or two at the railway station, which saves examination, and also some expense. A lumbering omnibus used to be the only conveyance waiting to take passengers into the town, which is half a mile distant. The road is bad and ill lighted.

Burgos to Madrid.—Railway—Dep. 4·30 A.M.　　Arr. 9·5 P.M.
　　Distance, **225** miles.　　　,, 5·46 P.M.　　 ,, 7·10 A.M.
　　Fare—160rs. (33*s*. 4*d*.)　　,, 11·9 ,,　　　,, 10·40 ,,
　　Time, 12 or 14 hours.

The mail-train, *direct* to Madrid, *leaves at* 11·9 P.M. If only going to *Valladolid*, take the 5·46 P.M. train. If stopping at *Venta de Banos* for *Leon*, it is better to leave Burgos at 4·30 A.M.

---

* At Alsasua the line is now open to Pamplona and Saragossa; but there are several changes by this route, and the trains are slow and uncertain.

Branch. | **Venta de Banos to Leon.**—Railway (viâ Palencia), two or three times daily.
Distance, 76 miles.
Fare, 59rs. 12c. (12s. 4d.) **LEON.** (Pop. 9800.) Hotel: *Parador del Norte.*
Time, 4¼ hours.

At 2·19 A.M. we arrive at

VALLADOLID. (Pop. 43,000; alt. 2100 ft.) Hotels: *Fonda del Norte, Fonda del Siglio de Oro*—the former is near the Railway Station, and very tolerable.

At 3·35 A.M. *Medina* for Salamanca.

Road. | **Medina to Salamanca.**—Diligences twice a day.
Distance, 43 miles. **SALAMANCA.** (Pop. 15,900.) Hotels:
Fare, 7ors. (14s. 6d.) *Posadas, de las Diligencias, de los Toros.*
Time, 8 hours.

At 9·6 A.M. the *Escorial* (seen from the railway); at 9·34 *Villalba,* the station for *Segovia* (for details see next page); at 10·40 A.M. *Madrid.*

MADRID. (Pop. about 300,000; alt. 2384 ft.) Hotels: *Grand Hôtel de Paris*, on the Puerta del Sol (*the best*); *Hôtel Péninsulaire*, 15, Calle Alcala; *Des Quatre Nations*, 10, Calle Mayor; *Los Principes*, well situated on the Puerta del Sol, and highly recommended, but we found it *dear,* and *not* first-rate. The *Inglaterra* has long been closed.

When the luggage has been examined by the Custom-house Officers (which takes some time) it is better not to take the omnibus, but send the luggage by it and go at once to the hotel in a cab (fare 4 rs.): you thus escape from the crowd of touters and beggars that infest all Spanish railway stations, and save half an hour's delay. The luggage will follow securely enough.* The charges for carriage and porterage of luggage are *everywhere most exorbitant,* always far exceeding the prices on the 'tarifs,' and those quoted in Guide-books generally.

Hotels in Madrid charge by the day for board and lodging, averaging 72rs. (15s.) each person, without wine or 'service,' and for poor apartments.

Couriers and *valets de place* are not only unnecessary but a nuisance in Madrid, where it is very easy to find one's way about. Do not be persuaded to take one to the 'Escorial,' or to Toledo, as *local guides are the best.*

Admirable large photographs of the pictures in the Museo have been lately taken by M. Laurent; they are to be purchased in Madrid, and at Marion's, Soho Square, London.

Madrid to Escorial.—Railway—Three trains daily.
Distance, 31½ miles. **ESCORIAL.**—Inn, *La Miranda.*
Fare, 22rs. 75c. (4s. 9d.) A local guide is necessary. Fee, 15 or 20 rs.
Time, 1½ hour.

---

* In case of any loss or delay, write at once to the *Office* of the 'Ferro Carril del Norte,' Calle Legatinos, 54, where the luggage will usually be found.

Madrid to Segovia.—Ry. to Villalba—Dep. 8 A.M. Arr. Vill. 10·15 A.M.
    Distance, about 50 miles.   ,, 2 P.M. ,, 3·11 P.M.
    Fare, 117rs. (24s. 5d.)   Diligence on arrival of first train.
    Time, 6 hours.   **SEGOVIA.**—(Pop. 118,298; alt. 3300.)
        Inns: *Café de la Plaza*; *Posada Nueva*.

N.B.—Do not attempt to return to Madrid by any other Route.

Madrid to Toledo.—Railway—Dep. 7 A.M.   Arr. 10 A.M.
    Distance, 56 miles.   ,, 6·15 P.M. ,, 9·10 P.M.
    Fare, 37rs. (7s. 9d.)   (Return trains at 6·10 A.M. and 6·25 P.M.)
    Time, 3 hours.   **TOLEDO.**—*Fonda de Lino*.

It is better to sleep at Toledo. A good guide at the hotel. If going further south, *return to Madrid first*. Change carriages at Aranjuez.

Madrid to Cordova.—Rly. to Venta ⎫ Dep. 7 A.M. Arr. Vta. Car. 5·10 P.M.
         de Cardenas. ⎭ ,, 8·55 P.M. ,, 5·47 A.M.
    Distance, 235 miles. (An interim of about sixty miles Diligence,
    Fare,* 300rs. (63s.)   then Ry. from Vilches to Cordova, see
    Time, 24 hours.   below.)

Take through tickets in Madrid at diligence offices.

The mail-train is at 8·55 P.M. There is no town of importance between Madrid and Cordova, and no place where you can well break the journey. It is better to *take provisions*. The French travelling 'buffets' are convenient and compact, and may be bought in Madrid.

Change carriages at Alcazar, where the train arrives at 1·15 A.M., the junction for *Valencia* and *Alicante*.

Branch from Alcazar.

  Madrid to Alicante.—Railway—Dep. 7 A.M.   Arr. 9·50 P.M.
    Distance, 282 miles.   ,, 8·55 P.M. ,, 11·11 A.M.
    Fare, 186 rs. 75 c. (39s.)   **ALICANTE.** (Pop. 31,000.) Hotel:
    Time, 15 hours.   *Fonda del Vapor*.

  Madrid to Valencia.—Rly.—{ As above to Alamansa, } Dep. 7 A.M. Arr. 11·10 P.M.
                            ,, 8·55 P.M. ,, 11·40 A.M.
    Distance, 297 miles.
    Fare, 201 rs. (42s.)   **VALENCIA.** (Pop. 126,000.) *Hotel*
    Time, 14 hours.   *de Paris, Fonda del Cid*.

Continuing the journey to *Cordova*, *Santa Cruz* is reached at 5 A.M. (the old terminus of this line), and at 6 A.M., *Venta de Cardenas*, where diligences both to Cordova and Granada meet the trains.

Departure, on arrival of train at 6 A.M., arriving at Vilches about 12 at noon.

    Vilches to Cordova—Rly.—Dep. 12·20 P.M.   Arr. 7·12 P.M. †

---

* The Fares to Cordova and Granada vary according to the demand for places.
† This train is very uncertain. The line between Vilches and Cordova has lately (April, 1866) been carried away by floods; there is one part, where no trains have been able to pass for months, in spite of the 'Indicador.'

CORDOVA. (Pop. 42,000.) Hotels: *Fonda Suiza, Fonda Rizzi*, both in the upper part of the town, in narrow streets; Fonda Suiza is the best, but there is a finer view from the back windows of the Fonda Rizzi. Here, as elsewhere in Spain, you must pay by the day. Take a local guide for the first day, and visit the mosque every *morning*.

Cordova to Seville.—Railway—Dep. 7·40 A.M.   Arr. 12·17 P.M.
Distance, 80 miles.   ,,   7·35 P.M.   ,,   11·40 A.M.
Fare, 52rs. 47c. (11s.)   ,,   8·15 ,,   ,,   12·25 ,,
Time, 4 hours.   (*Return trains at* 8·30 A.M. *and* 2·50 P.M.)

The Railway Stations are miserably appointed, both here and at Seville; at the latter the luggage is again examined.

SEVILLE. (Pop. 118,000.) Hotels: '*De Paris*,' good and dear; '*De Londres;*' '*De Madrid;*' '*De l'Europe*'—all central.

We found the Hôtel de Paris one of the best in Spain, very comfortable; but it was quite necessary to make an arrangement by the day.

A *valet de place* is useful for *one day*, as the streets are narrow, and some are very difficult to find. Remember to choose the brightest days to visit the Cathedral.

Seville to Cadiz.—Railway—Dep. 7 A.M.   Arr. 12 noon.
Distance, 94 miles.   ,,   12·10 P.M.   ,,   6·30 P.M.
Fare, 59rs. 70c. (12s. 6d.)
Time, 5 hours.   (*Return trains at* 7·20 A.M. *and* 8 P.M.)

Sit on the *right hand* of the railway carriage, to see the Bay of Cadiz.

CADIZ. (Pop. 71,500.) *Hôtel de Paris*, the best and most central, but *dear*, and in a narrow street; the *Hôtel Blanco*, on the 'Alameda,' is recommended, and has a fine sea-view.

The Railway Station is in the town, close to the port.

Steamers leave once or twice a week for Gibraltar and Malaga, and Gibraltar for Tangiers. They are regularly advertised. It is necessary to inquire about the steamers beforehand, as some are small, inconvenient, and hardly seaworthy in winter.

To Gibraltar, 7 or 8 hours. To Tangier from Gibraltar, about 4 hours.

Cadiz to Malaga (direct).—Steamer.—Lopez and Co.'s, every *Friday*,
Distance about 140 miles.   at 3 P.M.   (See Table at p. 248.)
Fare, 39frs. (31s. 2d.)   Take places, *at their Office*, several
Time, 14 to 16 hours.   days beforehand.
          Landing and embarking in small boats.

MALAGA. (Pop. 94,700.) Hotels: *Fonda de la Alameda*, on the Alameda, very good; *Hôtel Victoria*, kept by an Englishman, reasonable and comfortable.

There is a fixed tariff for landing luggage, passing it through the Custom-house, and for porterage to the hotels; but travellers are subject to much extortion. The luggage of 4 persons cost about 16s.—and nearly double was demanded—for a distance of 200 or 300 yards.

The same steamer leaves Malaga on Sunday at noon for Alicante (for Madrid), Barcelona, and Marseilles. (See Table at p. 248.)

[Malaga to Cordova—Railway—one train daily—line unfinished.]

Malaga to Gránada.—Diligences every day 3 P.M., Arr. 7 A.M.
Distance about 60 miles. There are several Companies. The 'Aliana' and the 'Madrilena' were the best. Secure places early.
Fare, 100rs. (21s.)
Time, 16 to 18 hours.

If a large party are going, it is better to hire a private omnibus, and take two days, sleeping at Loja. It is a very cold ride at night in winter, ascending nearly 3000 ft. from Malaga. The scenery is magnificent.

GRANADA. (Pop. 67,000; alt. 2445 ft.) Hotels: *Fonda de la Alameda*, good; *Fonda de la Victoria*, &c.

In *summer* stay for a few days at the '*Fonda de Ortiz*,' a small inn close to the walls of the Alhambra. The '*Fonda de los Siete Suelos*' is closed.

One of the best guides to the Alhambra is Emile Bensaken (père), to be heard of at the *Fonda de la Alameda*. The Palace is to be seen from 10 to 12, and from 2 to 4.

Visit the Gipsies' encampment, and witness their national dances.

Señ. Contrera's studio (the present restorer of the Alhambra) is also well worth a visit.

There are three routes to return to England:—

The First Route.—**Granada to Gibraltar (by Ronda)** on horseback.
Time, 4 or 5 days. Granada to Ronda about 34 miles. Ronda to San Roque, 80 miles.
(This journey cost a party of 7, with guides, 6l. each person in 1864. Scenery magnificent; accommodation rough.)
And from thence by P. and O. steamers to Southampton, which call off Gibraltar once a week. *Time*, average 6 days. Fare, 13l.

The Second Route.—By the coast of Spain. Return to Malaga by diligence, and take the steamer (Lopez and Co.) which leaves every Sunday for Marseilles, taking 4 or 5 days. Fare from Malaga to Marseilles, 180frs. (7l. 4s.) (See Table at p. 248.)

The Third Route is the following, as marked on the map.

Granada to Madrid.—Diligence and Rly. — Dil. to Venta de Cardenas daily, Rly. arr. at Madrid 9·40 P.M. next day. The '*Cordobesa*' and the '*Madrilena*' are the best appointed.
Distance, (abt.) 270 m.
Fare, 350rs. (73s. 6d.)
Time, about 32 hours.

The diligence portion of this journey still takes 22 hours.

Venta de Cardenas to } Railway—Dep. 11·16 A.M.   Arr. 9·40 P.M.
Madrid.   ,, 8·45 P.M.   ,, 6·40 A.M.
(Change carriages at Alcazar.)

Madrid to Saragossa.—Railway—Dep. 7.15 A.M.   Arr. 12 P.M.
Distance, 213½ miles.   ,, 8·25 P.M.   ,, 6·30 A.M.
Fare, 137rs. 75c. (28s. 9d.)
Time, 10 or 17 hours.   *(Return trains at 5 A.M. and 9·55 P.M.)*

If going direct, we recommend the night train, as the day journey is tiresome, and it is better to arrive at Saragossa by daylight.

SARAGOSSA. (Pop. 67,500.) Hotels: *De l'Univers* the best, and central. The *Hôtel de l'Europe* is in a more open situation.

Saragossa to Barcelona.—Railway—Dep. 3·27 A.M.   Arr. 4 P.M.
Distance, 226 miles.   ,, 8·20 A.M.   ,, 8·55 P.M.
Fare, 146rs. 14c. (30s. 6d.)
Time, 12 or 13 hours.   *(Return train at 7·30 A.M.)*

[At Zuera, 13 miles from Saragossa, there is a short route to Jaca and the Pyrenees, by Diligence and mule-path, taking 3 or 4 days. See O'Shea's, and Packe's, Guides.]

BARCELONA. (Pop. 183,900.) Hotels: *De las Cuatro Naciones* is good, and in the best situation; *Del Oriente; Café Sept Portes.*

Lopez and Co.'s Steamers leave here every week. See table at p. 248.

[Barcelona to Malaga. The railway to Valencia is now open (with a break of 4½ hours diligence); the route is well appointed.]

Barcelona to Perpignan.—Rly. to Gerona.—
Distance { Rly. to Ger., 61 m. } Dep. 6·30 A.M. Arr. Ger. 10·24 A.M.
          { Dil. to Perp., 47 m. } ,, 12·30 P.M.   ,, 4·28 P.M.
Fare, 115rs. (24s.)   ,, 5 P.M.   ,, 7·53 ,,
Time, about 18 hours.   Diligence on arrival of trains.

Take through tickets beforehand, in Barcelona, at Diligence Offices; those of '*El Comercio Rocellonés*' used to be the best.

The French frontier is reached at **PERPIGNAN** (Pop. 17,600), where all luggage is examined, and passports used to be required. Hotels: *Du Midi* and *Du Nord*.

Railway to Paris, viâ Marseilles or Bordeaux.

TABLE OF LOPEZ AND CO.'S STEAMERS.

Leave	Marseilles	... Tuesday,	11 A.M.	Leave Cadiz	...... Friday,	3 P.M.
Arrive at	Barcelona	... Wednesday.		Arrive at Malaga	..... Saturday.	
Leave	Do.	... Do.	3 P.M.	Leave Do.	...... Do.	Noon.
Arrive at	Alicante	..... Thursday.		Arrive at Alicante	..... Sunday.	
Leave	Do.	..... Saturday,	11 A.M.	Leave Do.	...... Wednesday,	11 A.M.
Arrive at	Malaga	...... Sunday.		Arrive at Barcelona	... Thursday.	
Leave	Do.	...... Do.	5 P.M.	Leave Do.	...... Do.	9 P.M.
Arrive at	Cadiz	.... Monday,	Morn.	Arrive at Marseilles	... Friday.	

	MARSEILLES.			MADRID.*			BARCELONA.			ALICANTE.			MALAGA.			CADIZ.		
Fares (in francs).	1st class.	2nd class.	3rd cls.	1st class.	2nd class.	3rd cls.	1st class.	2nd class.	3rd cls.	1st cls.	2nd cls.	3rd cls.	1st cls.	2nd cls.	3rd cls.	1st cls.	2nd cls.	3rd cls.
MADRID* ..	100	70	45	..	..	..	71	47	29	..	..	..	118	84	44	139	100	53
MARSEILLES.	..	..	..	100	70	45	55	37	18	95	63	37	179	121	61	205	137	70
BARCELONA.	55	37	29	71	47	29	..	..	..	63	42	24	134	89	45	161	108	55
ALICANTE ..	95	65	40	..	..	..	63	42	24	..	..	..	68	47	24	100	68	34
MALAGA ..	180	121	60	118	84	44	134	89	45	68	47	24	..	..	..	39	26	16
CADIZ	205	137	70	139	100	53	161	108	55	100	68	34	39	26	16	..	..	..

* Viâ Alicante.

SPANISH MONEY.

In commerce and in travelling, most calculations are made in '*reales*,' value 2½d. The coins in most frequent use are:—

Gold.....	The Doblon of	...	100 reales,	equal to	21s.	English.
,,	Duro (*Dollar*)	20	,,	,,	4s.	2d.	,,
Silver	,,	,,	,,	,,	,,	,,	,,
,,	Half ditto	10	,,	,,	2s.	1d.	,,
,,	Peseta	4	,,	,,	10d.	,,
,,	Reale		,,	,,	2½d.	,,
Copper ...	,,	Half Reale	,,	,,	,,	1¼d.	,,
	Tenth part of Reale						
	Cuarto, 8½ to reale—or 34½ to peseta.						

For convenience of calculation, 96 reales may be reckoned as equal to 1l. sterling, or 12 to 2s. 6d.; although bankers seldom give more than 95 to the 1l. in exchanging circular notes.

MEASUREMENT.

The modern Spanish league is equal to 3·45 statute, or 3 geographical, miles. The French kilomètre (5 furlongs) is the official measurement, and in use on railways.

GUIDE BOOKS.

Murray's Handbook (latest edition,	1861),	2 vols.	30s.	London.	J. Murray.
O'Shea's Guide to Spain	,,	,,	1865	1 vol.	15s.	,, Longman.
Packe's Guide to the Pyrenees	,,	1862	1 ,,	6s.	,,	,,
Itinéraire de l'Espagne, &c.	,,	1865	1 ,,	16½ frs.	Paris.	Hachette.
Revue des Musées d'Espagne	,,	1864	1 ,,	4 frs.	,,	Renouard.

LANGUAGE.

The French language is seldom spoken in Spain, excepting at Madrid; it is therefore *essential* for travellers to have some knowledge of Spanish.

www.ingramcontent.com/pod-product-compliance
Lightning Source LLC
Chambersburg PA
CBHW031333230426
43670CB00006B/332